FRENCH NOVELISTS, MANNERS AND IDEAS

*From the Renaissance
to the Revolution*

FRENCH NOVELISTS, MANNERS AND IDEAS

From the Renaissance
to the Revolution

FREDERICK C. GREEN

Professor Emeritus of French Literature
University of Edinburgh

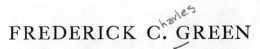

FREDERICK UNGAR PUBLISHING CO.
NEW YORK

Republished 1964
with some changes by the author

By arrangement with J. M. Dent & Sons Ltd.

First published 1929

Printed in the United States of America

Library of Congress Catalog Card No. 64-21610

INTRODUCTION

Was it not that most charming of French critics, M. René Doumic, who once remarked that anyone could write a novel? How very few, on the other hand, will undertake to define what a novel is. And, after all, if we consider the astonishing diversity, for example, in the works of two writers like Anatole France and Proust, it is clearly no easy matter to explain why we accord the common title of novelist to men so profoundly unlike in thought, in expression, in their attitude towards life and in their choice of subject-matter. Again, this business of definition is further complicated by the fact that the novel, the most recent and most prolific of all the forms of literature, is like a rising stream, inundating great stretches of territory hitherto regarded as well outside its reach. It was doubtless with this in mind that Anatole France predicted the speedy annexation by the novelist of the field of criticism, and indeed the trend of his own works provides a significant commentary to his statement.

Since definition implies a certain fixity in its object, and as the novel is such a kaleidoscopic form of literature, how are we to find a description sufficiently flexible and comprehensive to embrace the many and widely divergent species of this genre? Probably no definition can be free from objection, but the average reader's conception of the novel may perhaps be conveniently expressed in the following terms: A novel is a fictitious history related in prose, the purpose of which is to capture the interest by presenting a *probable* reflection of some aspect of life. As Brunetière pointed out, it is essentially an image of society. The aspect of life chosen for presentation, the manner in which it is projected, and the methods by which attention is drawn to the picture, are some of the primary factors to be discussed in considering the development of the modern novel.

The novel, in France as elsewhere, has never been, and can obviously never be, an absolutely national growth, and so, to understand the evolution of the French novel, we must, as in other forms of literature, examine the contribution made by the thought of foreign nations to the main current with which we are here concerned. As our knowledge of the history of literature extends, the starting-point of what is called the modern French novel is slowly receding. Twenty years ago, for instance, it was usual to point to the *Princesse de Clèves* as the first modern French novel. Later, however, when critics became more familiar with the works of seventeenth-century novelists, Mme de Lafayette was superseded by Honoré d'Urfé, whose *Astrée* was given the place of honour. Recent researches, particularly those of M. Reynier, show that the sixteenth century could boast of several works of a sentimental nature which fulfil most of the conditions required by our conception of what a novel ought to be.

A discussion of the sources of the modern French novel would necessitate a thorough examination of the origins of early verse-fiction. However, we may roughly classify this material under the heads *romans* and *fabliaux*. Usually both these forms of literature narrate physical adventures, but where the *romans* recount heroic and improbable exploits, the *fabliauxs* draw their material straight from everyday life and are in particular much concerned with sexual relations. Love would be too dignified a term to use in describing the themes of such productions. Some of Chaucer's coarser tales admirably illustrate the comic and erotic tendency of these French *fabliaux*. It will be seen that at the very inception of the modern French novel there are two well-defined tendencies, idealism and realism, and the history of the evolution of the French novel is really the account of the vicissitudes of these two great currents of human thought and action. Realism and idealism are of course to be found in every type of literature, but it is in the novel, which is *par excellence* the image of society, that it is possible to observe most clearly the interaction of these movements.

In the early stages of the development of realistic fiction in France, as in all western Europe, the comic intention is ever present, and one of the most interesting literary studies is offered by the novelist's changing attitude towards the common phenomena of life. Antoine de la Salle's *Petit Jehan de Saintré*, *Les Cent Nouvelles nouvelles*, and Rabelais' immortal *Pantagruel* and *Gargantua*, early prose narratives which are all lineal descendants of the old metrical *fabliaux*, reveal in their approach to the mysteries of birth and marriage a state of mind unclouded by philosophic doubt and free from metaphysical preoccupations. These *contes*, for they are not novels but disjointed narratives of a purely descriptive sort, continued for many years to delight all classes of society. In the seventeenth century such *joyeusetés* were still popular, and those who did not or could not enjoy them in book form went to the fairs and heard the side-splitting patter of mountebanks, like the famous Tabarin, who embodied the funniest of these episodes in their entertainments. The *joyeusetés* or *facéties* are, in embryo, realistic or satirical novels, but it was not until the seventeenth century that they acquired that unity of interest which is so essential to the novel and which alone can give the reader the illusion that he is observing a phase of life.

CONTENTS

CONTENTS

FRENCH NOVELISTS, MANNERS AND IDEAS

RENAISSANCE TO THE REVOLUTION

CHAPTER I

THE IDEALISTIC NOVEL

CHRONOLOGICALLY at least, the romantic novel, in point of development, takes precedence over the novel of real life. The reason for this is not far to seek. Paradoxical as it may sound, it is easier to imagine than to describe, and the readiest way to interest man is to appeal to his fancy. Probability is, after all, an acquired taste and a comparatively recent one in the history of fiction. One has only to reflect on the predominance of purely imaginative literature in the Middle Ages to realise that the novelist and the poet were begotten by the same Muse. It is not surprising, then, to discover that in the sixteenth century the romantic novel is already an accomplished fact in France. The term "romantic" is of course unsatisfactory, since it is ambiguous. In this connection the French language is richer than ours, and differentiates between the *roman romanesque* and the *roman romantique*, the product of that nineteenth-century literary movement which we call Romanticism. A better though not wholly acceptable adjective for the novel which makes no attempt to adhere to the facts of real life would be "idealistic." The expression has the advantage of being sufficiently ample to embrace three types of novel which reached a fairly advanced stage of evolution in the sixteenth century: the chivalrous, the tragic and the sentimental novel.

The novel of chivalry is the offspring of the mediaeval epic, the *roman breton* and the *chanson de geste*, those tales of courtly love, of enchantment and of knightly prowess, a species of literature common to all western Europe, and which the great Spaniard Cervantes attacked but did not quite destroy in his immortal *Don Quijote*. The reaction against this sort of fiction was represented in France by *Le petit Jehan de Saintré*, of which mention has been already made. A further lease of life indeed was given to this type of literature by the French translation of the famous *Amadis de Gaule*, whose hero is the prototype of the constant knightly lover who devotes his wandering life to the succour of fair maidens in distress. Des Essar's version of the *Amadis* appeared in 1540, and was eagerly read. Yet it cannot be said that the chivalrous novel was entirely free from realism, for ever and anon it reveals disconcerting flashes of brutal reality and evidence of a gross conception of love which is strangely at variance with the general tenor of this kind of tale.

The *Amadis* is of Spanish origin, and represents only a small part of the contribution made by Spain to the French novel. When we examine the beginnings of the French novel of sentiment, we shall see that Italy too was called upon for material. The chivalrous novel, with its stock situation, love in distress rescued by a respectful and doughty hero, maintained itself throughout the whole of the sixteenth century and well into the seventeenth before succumbing to the demands of outraged reason. If we examine the bibliographies of French late sixteenth-century novels, we notice that the chivalrous novel flourished chiefly between 1590 and 1610. Their titles are significant: *Chastes amours*, *Amours et fortunes guerrières*, *Les divers effets de l'amour*, *Les alarmes de l'amour* well describe the matter which popular novelists like Du Perier, De Nervèze and Nicolas de Montreux offered to a credulous and receptive public.

But already, in the thirties of the sixteenth century, the influence of that great artist Boccaccio began to filter into France by way of translations of the *Decameron* and of *Fiammette*. The French version of Alberti's *Hecatomphile* (1534) also did much to accustom readers to a more subtle conception of love as something not wholly physical and yet less nebulous than the phantom idea presented by the chivalrous novel. The passion of love, its cruelty and its misery, were new ideas which fertilised the French novel. The fact that these new and illuminating aspects of life were enshrined in a familiar, everyday setting contributed greatly to their popularity, and helped to advance the evolution of the novel in France. In the light of developments which were to ensue in the seventeenth century, the additional contributions made by the Spanish novelists are most instructive. In contradistinction to the somewhat easy virtue of Boccaccio's heroines, the women created by San Pedro (1526) in his *Prison d'amour*, and by Flores in his *Jugement d'amour* (1530), reveal a resistance to amorous advances somewhat akin to the attitude portrayed in the old French courtly epic. The keynote of these Spanish works is sacrifice, but it is always the man who is the victim, a theme which, as we shall see, was destined to become famous in the French novel of the early seventeenth century. Another outstanding characteristic of the Spaniards is the prominence they gave to brutal descriptions of the tragic effects of unhappy love, a morbid strain which we shall repeatedly catch in French fiction.

Possibly the first French novel to betray the fusion of these foreign influences with native inherited material is from the pen of a lady called Helisienne de Crenne. Her *Angoysses douleureuses qui procèdent d'amour* (1538) is to some extent reminiscent of Boccaccio's *Griselda* and *Fiammette*. It is the story of the struggles waged by a married woman against an overmastering passion for a man of humble birth. The novel rises in an admirable crescendo to the climax where the long-suffering husband locks his wife up in a castle. Unfortunately the high promise of the first part is not sustained, and the lover, hitherto represented as a flippant Adonis, blossoms out into

the typical chivalrous hero who kills the trouble-
some husband and arrives in time to hear from the
lips of his chaste mistress a full dying renunciation
of all her adulterous thoughts. Nevertheless, from the
point of view of characterisation, this novel shows the
beginnings of the analytic novel of sentiment. Love
is no longer the servant of desire, since our heroine,
though rather thanks to marital vigilance than to
good intention, does not consummate her passion.
The novel is situated in a bourgeois setting, another
contribution to the development of probability.

A French novelist who hid his identity behind the
pseudonym of Théodose Valentinian produced in 1555
a novel of tragic love entitled *L'Amour ressuscité de
la mort d'amour*. It is the story of a man who becomes
secretly engaged to a girl and who, whilst in England
upon a diplomatic mission, is stunned by the news
that the lady has married another man. The cadre
of the novel, the convincing nature of the adventures
related, render it most unusual and precocious. Incidentally, readers of *The Cloister and the Hearth* will
recognise in the episode of the terrified Jew, who
when in danger of shipwreck vows a statue to Saint
Christopher, a verbatim translation of a scene from
Valentinian's tale. The complete absence of any
motive for the heroine's apostasy is typical of the
lack of psychology which we find in Spanish models,
yet the French author has caught one admirable
Spanish trait in his expression of tragic love. It is
something, too, at this period to escape the eroticism
of the Italian school and of the *fabliaux*.

The disturbed social atmosphere of the civil wars was hardly favourable to the development of analysis of sentiment in the French novel of this time. The public turned rather to the chivalrous novel, with its accounts of physical action, and to the Rabelaisian *conte*, which was absorbing new vigour from the Italians Straparola, Domenchi and Aretino. The French novel was evolving, however, in respect to setting and background, and whilst no great development was to be observed in the treatment of the love theme, we may notice in the imitations of Greek novels an effort to enhance the interest of stock situations by placing them in foreign climes. Again, in Belleforest's popular adaptations of the short stories of the Italian Bandello, we have the first intimation of the appearance of the *nouvelle* which took its theme, generally a tragic one, straight from the events of contemporary life and framed it in a pseudo-historical setting, an interesting example of a new sort of realism free from all comic intent and not at all lacking in probability.

But we have digressed for a moment from the novel of pure imagination in which the study of sentiment has begun to preoccupy the author, though scarcely at a moment seasonable for the growth of such a tendency. But the comparative calm which followed the promulgation of the Edict of Nantes made possible the existence of a cultured society clique, and a brilliant coterie of noblewomen which included the Princess Margaret of Lorraine and the Duchess of Retz, soon made its influence felt in literary circles. In the early years of the seventeenth century Marguerite de Valois attracted many novelists to her *salon* in Paris, where the future marquise de Rambouillet, that queen of *précieuses*, doubtless conceived the idea of her celebrated *chambre bleue*. Women became now powerful in French aristocratic society, and morally, at least, their influence on the novel was wholesome. As always, high morality in literature is purchased at a price, as will become evident in the subsequent history of the idealistic school of fiction.

If we look at the trappings of the chivalrous novel at the close of the sixteenth century we can discern changes of a drastic sort. *Don Quijote* had not yet appeared to laugh the *merveilleux* out of court, but already, in the *Mille imaginations de Cypille* (1609), we find a travesty of the *mise en scène* of the chivalrous novel; and in several other works novelists try to substitute an historical French background for the old one. In some, however, probability was cast to the winds in an effort to stimulate the interest by descriptions of strange lands, an interesting development foreshadowing the coming vogue for the oriental or exotic setting which the French have always loved in their fiction. But soon an intrinsic progress becomes also evident. The revolution in the relations between men and women found a reflection in the novelist's treatment of love, which gradually became more and more refined until, having lost all its physical attributes, it threatened to develop into purely metaphysical passion. The platonic conception of love, entering France by way of Italy, encountered a society in full reaction against the exaggerated licence of past literature. It was this sentiment, tinged with the gloom of the old Spanish novel and saved from austerity by the graceful voluptuousness of Boccaccian memories, which formed the core of the dawning novel of sentiment. M. Reynier indicates the period 1594–1610 as the dawn of this new type of fiction. He notices very acutely that the married woman was now replaced as heroine by the young girl, a fact which seems to show that the novelist, subtle as he was, had yet much to learn about the possibilities latent in situations like that later exploited by Madame de Lafayette. But though in places these novels reveal the promise of advance in the art of characterisation and in the analysis of sentiment, they are still overloaded with much irrelevant incident and mythological rubbish. Love is sterilised out of all probability. Lovers discuss their passion with complete detachment and in conformity with the rules of a dialectic which any curious inquirer may find in the copious manuals of the day. Excellent practice in analysis though this was, it was so completely divorced from the reality of human passion as to deprive these novels of any interest. The novelist, by reflecting the love-making of a society and literary set where the paying of court was a finicky process governed by protocol, retarded the evolution of the psychological novel of sentiment for a period of nearly sixty years.

What then may conveniently be called the inner

evolution of the idealistic novel betrays a slight but perceptible forward movement during the first decade of the sixteenth century. In other respects also, important changes are taking place. It is clear that the novelist, despite the improbability of his conception of love, has begun to reflect at least one aspect of social life, and curiously enough it is his fidelity to this purpose which alienates the novel from life as a whole. His error is the common one noticeable even in the twentieth century of selecting a top stratum instead of a cross-section of life for presentation.

Now that small but powerful group of fashionable intelligentsia, the *arbitri elegantiarum*, who had revolutionised the novelist's attitude towards sentiment, gradually evinced a desire to escape still more completely from the realities of life. It was natural that, following upon a period of internecine strife, the French should have experienced a certain war weariness: it was natural too that this feeling should find expression in a hankering after an illusory golden age. This indefinable longing was reflected in the novel, which proceeded to stage its adventures in a pastoral setting reminiscent of the cadre affected by Theocritus in his idylls and by Vergil in his eclogues. It will be remembered that the old Greek novels of the *Daphnis and Chloe* type had enjoyed a certain vogue at the close of the sixteenth century, when they were wafted into France on the warm zephyr of Humanism. Indeed, models were not lacking, since the Spanish *Diane* by Montemayor had appeared as recently as 1578. Such pastoral literary productions, or *bergeries*, after a period of great popularity on the stage, passed over into the new genre, where they met with an equally enthusiastic reception. Apart from the actual background, these novels reveal another point of difference from the chivalrous novel. The incidents are no longer warlike and heroic, but more in conformity with the growing gentleness in manners. One of the earliest critics of the French novel, Charles Sorel, himself a writer of repute, notes in 1664 that the pastoral novel, *le roman berger*, represented an effort on the part of the novelist to respond to an increasing demand for greater probability in fiction. If we examine the archetype of the French seventeenth-century pastoral novel it will be seen that Sorel's judgment was correct.

L'Astrée, by Honoré d'Urfé, first began to appear in 1610 and continued to delight the public for well-nigh a century, long after the vogue for the pastoral had vanished. It is the story, in a fictitious fifth-century setting, of the love affairs of the shepherds Céladon and Astrée, but D'Urfé makes it quite clear from the outset that his nymphs, shepherds, shepherdesses and druids are conventional masks, and it needs no acumen to discern behind the tissue of fiction a picture of the manners of French seventeenth-century aristocratic society. The *Astrée* captures all the streams which we have indicated in tracing the main current of the French novel of pure imagination. Spain, Italy, ancient Greece and Rome and mediaeval France all contributed to this twelve-volume work of fiction which marks an epoch in the history of the French novel.

D'Urfé's style, his chiefest charm, is as limpid as the River Lignon on whose banks the pretty love scenes have their being. The Forez, which the author knew from childhood, is the country where these refined shepherds pass the halcyon days in elegant, leisurely talk, sifting through the delicate sieve of analysis the myriad sentiments inspired by an intercourse between the sexes which is lifted above the drossy facts of ordinary carnal love. As in the old chivalrous novel, the hero is governed in all his conduct by an ideal and highly moral code which forbids him to hope for reward. He is the slave of his lady's caprice and is skilled in the art of dialectic which takes the place of the mediaeval knight's physical prowess. As one great critic has pointed out, there is hardly a single variety of love which is not dissected in the *Astrée*. But in places there are rents in the gauzy envelope which reveal the existence of a mode of life less ideal, it is true, but more in keeping with probability. The Daphnides and Délies occasionally descend from the rarefied upper ether to solid earth, and the malicious Hylas, the bad shepherd, is there to remind us that there were even in the aristocratic society of the reign of Henri IV. certain limits to the upward flight of idealism.

D'Urfé's technique represents an advance in the evolution of the art of the novel. His *Astrée* is fairly well constructed, since despite its numerous digressions and intercalated episodes it has a definite plot, and it is something to discover a novel at this time with a beginning, a middle and an end. The *dénouement*, it is true, is still dependent on the *merveilleux*, that fairy-tale element which persists so long in French fiction. Again, if we accept the platonic conception of love which impregnates the *Astrée*, the conduct of the characters is consistent. Their actions are of course dictated by a fixed code, and it is this which imparts so much monotony to the tale. However, the author stimulates the interest by means of a hundred little descriptive touches, and these lend individuality to some of his creations. It must not be forgotten, too, that they are modelled on historical figures like Marguerite de Valois, Henri IV., and in the case of the doubting Hylas the author himself is said to be the original.

The success of the *Astrée* was immense. It was the *livre de chevet* of every well-known character in French seventeenth-century society, and its fame spread even to the wilds of Germany. In England, however, its popularity was not very great if we are to judge by translations: this is possibly due to the fact that in Sidney's *Arcadia* that country already possessed a very excellent pastoral novel of its own. In France, where the *Astrée* sounded the keynote to which polite society attuned its conversation, one immediate result of its influence was the founding of the first real *salon*, and one which was destined to achieve a doubtful fame thanks to the raillery of Molière. Catherine de Vivonne, marquise de Rambouillet, like so many other intelligent women, found in the æsthetic doctrines of Honoré a tranquil and intellectual enjoyment which was as balm to a mind distracted by the brutality of the late civil wars. The witty ladies and gentlemen who foregathered in the famous *chambre bleue* to exchange ideas must not be judged by their unworthy imitators, those *pecques provinciales* immortalised by Molière. Voiture, Chapelain, Ménage, and two women whose influence on the novel was important—Mlle de Scudéry and Mme de Lafayette—all to some extent formed their minds in the Hôtel de Rambouillet. It has become the fashion to ridicule D'Urfé's idealism: this contempt was shared by his contemporaries, as is the fate of every admirable movement that tends to depart too far from the humdrum of real life.

The *Astrée* produced a host of imitations, but amongst these none which, as Voltaire would have put it, show how the original ought to have been written. The ponderous Gomberville, who spent what time he had left from novel-writing in a vain attempt to hunt the inoffensive conjunction *car* from the French language, showed in his *Carithée* (1621) what the pastoral novel can become in the hands of a pedant. The book, he tells us, is a *roman à clef* in which Charles IX. is portrayed as a shepherd lover. His swains are, however, fatuous, and, unlike D'Urfé's, are poor conversationalists. They appear to spend their time either mooning round disconsolately or else indulging in a sort of game of catch in which wooden bowls symbolise hearts and which are airily tossed to and fro to the refrain " Je te donne mon cœur!" But Gomberville, in his *Polexandre* (1632), struck out in a new direction, for his novel from the point of view of setting reveals an attempt to break with the pastoral cadre by transporting the action to exotic lands. It is indeed a crude effort to introduce local colour by describing foreign *mœurs* — a sort of applied geography. One critic looks on Gomberville as a precocious Loti: one might also discern in him an ancestor of the author of *Salammbô*. In this fruitful period much was being done in an experimental way to arouse interest by similar methods; it is a period of purely external development since, as we have seen, the essence of the novel, i.e. the part concerned with the analysis of sentiment, is moving but slowly. Already in 1627 a strange character called De Gerzan, half scientist, half alchemist, had tried, in a series of histories named after the four known continents, to make the novel a vehicle for scientific propaganda. In these queer pastoral-heroic productions he claimed to respect probability both in chronology and in geography, and to preserve at the same time complete unity of plot. De Gerzan is worth mentioning as an example of the many good intentions which litter the prefaces of seventeenth- and eighteenth-century novels, intentions which unfortunately were rarely put into practice.

It becomes evident in works like *La Fille supposée* (1635), *La Princesse inconnue* (1635), and in Du Bail's most un-Chinese *Fameux Chinois* (1642), that the pastoral *motif* is doomed. The matter which composes the intrigue of such novels has been summed up

very well by one of the authors in his sub-title:
"disguises, combats, jealousies, the passion of love
and hate, constancy and infidelity." If we throw
in abductions and wicked husbands, it will be seen
that the novel of sentiment and adventure which
we noticed in the sixteenth century is beginning to
threaten the supremacy of the novel of idealised
love. And though the hero still expresses himself
in the old flowery language, he is human enough to
demand some tangible guerdon from the owner of
the "bouche de roses" and the "beau sein de lys"
before swearing complete submission to the lady's
will. Still, the *chambre bleue* carried the day and the
cult of the *bel esprit* prevailed in the novel, though
the platonic love-making was transported indoors.
Already evident in *Carithée*, a mania for antiquity
had arisen, and soon the Alcidors and Céladons were
to cast aside their crooks and goatskins for the
martial javelin and casque of the heroes of ancient
history.

That gallant gentleman La Calprenède, author of
several historical tragedies, produced in his *Cassandre*
(1642–5) a novel which reflects admirably the new
taste. Its central theme is the love of the Scythian
Oroondate for the Princess Statira (Cassandre), the
daughter of Darius. But the real hero is the mighty
Alexander, the very pattern of valour, generosity
and elegance, *l'homme galant* dear to the ladies of
the *chambre bleue* and to the neo-*précieuses* who frequented the Saturdays of Mlle de Scudéry. Here, as
in that farrago of ancient history and fiction which

he called *Cléopâtre* (1647), La Calprenède, despite his prolixity, preserves some coherence both in plot and in characterisation. Indeed, the gallant Artaban, the embodiment of fearless pride, is boldly drawn and thrilled a company which but a few years before had eagerly responded to the proud note sounded by Corneille in his *Cid*. Some maintain that seventeenth-century tragedy and the more romantic tragi-comedy are the offspring of the heroic novel of adventure, but without entering into the very delicate question of priority in two genres which were constantly interfluent, we can see that the society of 1650 wanted more physical action in its fiction. This does not mean that the old *Astrée* conception of love was abandoned by the novelist: it still remained a respectful sentiment which subjected its slaves to feminine tyranny. In fact, the moral ascendancy of the Frenchwoman in literature was never so complete as during the period beginning with the Fronde and ending with the seventeenth century. One has only to skim through the heroic novels of La Calprenède's imitators, Chevreau, Vaumorière, Le Vayer de Boutigny and Mlle de Senecterre, to find that all the deeds of valour they relate are mere tributes to the feminist cult. With Mlle de Gournay writing on the "Egalité des femmes et des hommes," with Mlle Guillaume proving from ancient history the undoubted superiority of woman, and that extraordinary Amazon La Grande Mademoiselle striding from the camp into the *salon*, small wonder if the novelist trimmed his sails to the new breeze.

Somewhere, in speaking of French eighteenth-century literature, Brunetière, prince of critics, deplores the results of feminine influence and maintains that when a nation writes for feminine applause it writes below its best. It is perhaps significant that the heroic novel as exemplified in the works of its greatest exponent, Mlle Scudéry, represents no great progress in those profound elements which we associate with excellence in prose fiction, probability and psychology. It is true that in the fabulation of *Le Grand Cyrus* and *Clélie* Madeleine was aided by her brother, who was a swashbuckler and a fool. But in the conversations which constitute the chief attraction of *Cyrus* there is a dreadful lack of verbal economy, an irritating old-maidishness and a harping prudery which outdo even Richardson in his *Grandison*. Sorel, writing in 1664, tells us that *Cyrus* delighted contemporaries by its picture of fashionable life, and a nineteenth-century critic saw in it a disguised history of the Fronde.

The first tome of *Cyrus* appeared in 1649 and the tenth in 1653. Its great length and its interminable recitals of improbable events did not terrify the reader of the seventeenth century, whose leisure was plentiful and who had not grown blasé with surfeit of fiction. Each volume was eagerly scanned for its "portraits" or descriptive sketches of well-known society people. Victor Cousin discovered a key to this novel, and we know that Artamène or Cyrus was Condé; Mandane, Mme de Longueville; Cléomère, la marquise de Rambouillet; and ironically enough the

ugly Madeleine herself was that Sapho of whom it
was written at her death—

> Cy-git la Sapho de nos jours,
> Qui, sur la Grecque eut l'avantage
> D'accorder les tendres amours
> Avec la raison la plus sage.

Such portraits became the rage but we would do
well to listen to M. Lebreton's warning before accept-
ing them as historical documents. Yet, in one respect,
they show development in the novel which, by becoming a reflection of one facet of society, moves
closer to probability. Of psychology, that is, analysis
of motives leading to conduct, there is little or none
in *Cyrus*, but Sorel looked on the pseudo-historical
setting as an attempt to make the novel more probable, and, after all, probability is a relative quantity
dependent on the extent of the reader's knowledge.

We need not try to follow Artamène through the
maze of his ten-thousand-page pursuit of the elusive
Mandane. It is enough to know that, after having
been satisfied, from innumerable conversations and
letters, as to the propriety of his intentions, Mandane
coyly consents to marriage, and the swooning lover,
overcome by his unexpected good fortune, has to be
supported by two squires on the staircase which
leads to my lady's chamber.

The interest of *Clélie* (1654–60) lies in the well-
known *Carte de Tendre* which maps out the route to
be followed by the constant and gentlemanly lover
who would aspire to the affections of a *précieuse*. The
adventures which happen to the hero Aronce before

his marriage with Clélie are a repetition of the sort related in *Cyrus*, or indeed in any other heroic novel of the time. The idea of the *Carte de Tendre* is briefly this: *Tendre* signifies broadly love, or at least the *précieuse* conception of the highest degree of sentiment which a lady may properly entertain for a suitor. There are three towns of this name situated on three different rivers: *Tendre sur Estime*, the first, may be attained after passing through the villages of *Grand Esprit*, *Jolis Vers*, *Billets Galants*, mounting through *Respect* to the goal. This road, though long, is passable by all. The same is true of *Tendre sur Reconnaissance*, which is reached through *Complaisance*, *Soumission*, *Petits Soins*, etc., if one avoids such pitfalls as *Négligence* and *Indifférence*. The most difficult of access is, however, *Tendre sur Inclination*, which is reserved for the elect. Here there are no intermediate stages but the great danger of being swept on by the torrent of inclination to the uncharted sea, *La Mer dangereuse*, beyond which lie unknown regions fatal to virtue. I do not know whether it has been pointed out that there is a striking resemblance between the progress of Mlle. de Scudéry's constant lover and that of Bunyan's hero. Apart altogether from the difference in their aspirations, the allegorical or symbolic procedure is the same, though of course it is quite unlikely that Sapho had ever heard of Bunyan. The allegory was sufficiently well known in old French literature to suggest at once the source of Scudéry's idea. Indeed, Sorel formally says that the French *cartes* owed nothing to English productions of a similar sort. The conversational possibilities of the *Carte de Tendre* were immense and, from Scudéry's own *salon* to every establishment of the kind founded in the provinces, the doctrine of *honnête amitié* was analysed and commented upon. It became, says one critic, a sort of drawing-room game, and it is easy to imagine what a piquant stimulus to conversation must have been afforded by the personal applications arising from this ingenious device.

Before summing up the contribution made to the evolution of the novel by the *roman parfait* or *roman héroïque*, let us turn for a moment to a new tendency which arose in the idealistic novel without, however, producing immediate results. The Church, as is well known, has always kept a vigilant eye on new types of French literature. The theatre had frequent and sharp reminders of this fact. The novel, because of its widespread popularity, soon attracted the attention of clerics, many of whom would gladly have stamped it out of existence. Camus, the genial bishop of Belley, the flail of the monks, conceived the saner plan of diverting the novel from its wicked ways by substituting for profane love the more ideal theme of spiritual love. Camus is to some extent the father of the *roman - feuilleton*. He loved the sensational, and like Pickwick's fat boy yearned to make his auditor's flesh creep. He annexed the melodramatic baggage of the sixteenth-century tale of tragedy and passion, but instead of bringing about his *dénouement* by marriage he made his heroines end by being con-

verted. For him any means were good which justified
the didactic and moral purpose, and his startling titles,
La Courtisane solitaire, *Elise ou l'Innocence coupable*,
are in the best tradition of the servant-girl novelette
literature of Victorian England. His novels, from the
theological point of view, were questionable, and
might not have met with the approval of the peevish
ascetic, but they were an immense success with the
public of the first half of the seventeenth century.

If we retrace rapidly the evolution of the idealistic
novel, it will be seen that advance has been made
towards greater probability. Successive types of
novel reveal modifications which respond to an increasing demand for verisimilitude. The *romans de
chevalerie*, with their astounding tales of enchantment,
made way for the gentler and more likely situations
of the pastoral. With Scudéry the heroic novel,
while still retaining exaggerated and impossible
adventures, made these an excuse for a passable
picture of contemporary manners, and the conventional and transparent veil of pseudo-classic history
did not seem odd to a society accustomed to the
same antique setting in Racinian tragedy. The "portraits," too, were sketched in detail and the physiognomy and costume carefully described. If the psychological traits strike us as vaguely limned, remember
that we are dealing with a period where mankind
and not the individual is the consecrated subject of
all literary genres, and that the writer is content to
outline boldly the essential characteristics of each
vice and virtue before incorporating them in the

composite creation he calls a *caractère*. That novels, and very good ones, can be composed in this way, we know. But that minute portrayal of the origins of such characteristics, and that fascinating recital of their reactions to the various circumstances of everyday life which we have grown accustomed to in the modern novel, are but dimly foreshadowed in the French novel of the mid-seventeenth century. Yet, if we overlook his stereotyped treatment of love, the novelist did endeavour to approach reality, though the reality in this case was a false one; but he forgot that there was another France outside the walls of the Hôtel de Rambouillet: the France of the bourgeoisie and the people. But here were subjects too crude for the delicate texture of romantic fiction, which demanded the coarser and more homely fabric of the satiric novel.

CHAPTER II

IRONICALLY enough, it was D'Urfé himself who was indirectly the cause of the reaction against the pastoral novel, though indeed such a reaction was inevitable. By creating in the *Astrée* the character of Hylas, the faithless, mocking shepherd, he suggested to a certain Prudent Gauthier the idea for his *Mort d'Amour*, or "the real and new history of the amours of Calianthe and Florifile." Taking as his model this very Hylas, Gauthier made of him a cynical seducer whose object in life is to avoid acquiring that reputation for fidelity which is the hall-mark of the pastoral lover. Gauthier's style is a curious mixture of refined sensualism and popular coarseness. Whilst preserving the outward form of the *Astrée*, he describes the gross and realistic love affairs of his hero with Jeanneton, a real shepherdess. He is, in short, the author of the first *anti-roman*. Gauthier's book, which appeared in 1616, does not seem to have attracted much attention, doubtless because of the continued success of the *Astrée*.

We must remember that in the farces and in the popular *contes* which flourished at this time there was ample pabulum for those grosser minds which

23

failed to appreciate the elegant idealism of the pastoral novel. Again, ever since the beginning of the century, the brutal and cynical adventures of the Spanish picaresque novel had been known to the French in translations of *Guzman d'Alfarache* (1600) and *Lazarille de Tormes* (1601). In his reactionary attempt on the *Astrée*, too, Gauthier had before him the successful example of Cervantes, whose immortal satire on another sort of idealistic novel, the novel of chivalry, had been rendered into French by Oudin in 1614. Thus there were three distinct types of fiction which, however much they differed in subject-matter, had at least one thing in common. The adventures of the picaro, the homely grossness of the *conte*, and the pitiless mockery of *Don Quijote*, all appealed to the most accessible of the sentiments: the sense of humour. One has only to consider the numbers of reprints of such books which kept on appearing till the end of the century to realise their popularity. And the success of *Gil Blas*, which happily blended the best features of such productions, was the inevitable result of a steadily growing taste for comic adventures of a probable kind.

Whilst all such novels are essentially satirical, the purpose of the satire varies. Sometimes it is political, sometimes social. All are inimical to idealism, but the *anti-roman*, the greatest example of which we are about to discuss, is deliberately levelled at the idealistic novel then in vogue: the pastoral. The interesting feature of this movement is the conscious effort to bring the novel closer to the realities of life.

But as is the case with most reactionary attempts, the object is sometimes not attained. Satire, particularly when it degenerates into burlesque, can lead a novelist as far from reality as the most unbridled idealism. This, as we shall see, was one of the defects of the new type of fiction which found its first important representative in Charles Sorel, the author of two novels, *Francion* (1623) and *Le Berger extravagant ou l'Anti-roman* (1627).

Brunetière sought to explain the comparative failure of the French novel of the seventeenth century by saying that it had no consciousness of its function or of its purpose. Yet if we read the literary reminiscences of Sorel, or if we examine the prefaces of early seventeenth-century novels, the contrary seems to be the case. "Good comic or satirical novels," says Sorel, "seem more than any other to be reflections of history, and since they take as their subject the common actions of life they approach more closely to truth." Humanity appeared to him, as to Molière, to be more prone to folly than to wisdom, and the comic novel suggested itself to Sorel as an admirable instrument for social satire. Indeed, if the device "castigat ridendo mores" should have become associated with comedy rather than with the novel in seventeenth-century France, it is due more to lack of genius than to an absence of intention on the part of the novelist.

The love of Francion, a young French country gentleman of good family, for a romantic Italian lady called Naïs provides Sorel with an excuse for a satirical novel of manners. He boasted that he had put the whole French language into his *Francion*, and the diversity of pictures presented certainly demands a vocabulary of exceptional range. *Francion* is a realistic account of the manners of the French bourgeoisie and petty nobility in the early years of the seventeenth century. It also provides glimpses into the lower world, the habitat of the Grisons and Rougets, the French counterparts of the Spanish picaro, and the life-history of the old hag Agathe reveals the existence of a class which preys on the wealthy bourgeois and gullible squire. For the modern reader the obscenities and coarse practical jokes which compose the first book are interesting merely because they indicate the sources from which Sorel drew so generously, the popular *fabliaux* and Spanish picaresque novel. But *Francion* is the first French novel of school life. The college of Lisieux, where the irrepressible hero is flogged and starved into a hardened scamp, is vividly described. Sorel's style is slovenly. He has little idea of varying his conversation to suit his characters, but by sheer garrulity he succeeds in detaching from a mass of detail the unforgettable picture of Hortensius, fool, pedant, miser and usher. His credulity makes him the butt of delighted youth. The turmoil of the classroom, theatre of that eternal battle between scholar and *pion*, re-echoes through the early pages of *Francion*. The regent, an egregious idiot, looms ever in the background, whip in hand. "Quelle vilenie!" exclaims the author, to see the education of youth entrusted to

ignorant bumpkins who, by a smattering of knowledge of the commentaries of the scholiasts, succeed
in eventually acquiring an M.A. Sorel is a social
reformer, and spares us no detail which will make
his thesis complete. "Our plan is to see a picture
of human life," he explains, "so that we must show
here the various documents." It will be seen, therefore, that he joins hands in intention at least with
the realists of the nineteenth century.

It is unfortunate that Sorel is so didactic. At every
stage he stops to explain his procedure and his purpose. Obsessed with the importance of his self-inflicted
rôle as a social reformer, he continually harps on the
corrective value of his work, but does not scruple to
resort to licentiousness in order to pad out his tale.
As he confesses, the most serious matters are used by
him as material for farce. The law, medicine, the
Church become the object, not of satire, but of buf-
foonery. Yet even here he is inconsistent, for it is
clear that *Francion* was not composed at a single
stroke. The original audacity of the anti-clerical part
is gradually toned down under the influence, one
feels, of some strong external pressure, and it is
something of an anti-climax when we find our author
rebuking one of his characters for heresy in speaking
ill of the priesthood.

Sorel is at home when he amuses himself at the
expense of authors and booksellers. He is very scorn-
ful of the popular novelist, with his "pourpoint de
l'Héliotrope," his "jarretières de Céladon," and his
"rose à la Parthenice," who yet is not ashamed to

make money by his pen. For the bourgeois he has great sympathy, and is furious that the word should have become an insult in Paris. A country wedding, a rustic wooing, a *conseiller au parlement de Bretagne* are subjects which Sorel loves to describe, and there is a sympathetic quality about this aspect of his *Francion* which reveals the possibility of a distinctively French novel reflecting provincial manners. He did not, however, exploit this promising lode. His fertile mind, preoccupied with the idea of writing a novel as diametrically opposed as possible to the ideal type of fiction represented by the *Astrée*, and attracted doubtless by the success achieved by *Don Quijote*, conceived the *Berger extravagant*, a travesty of the pastoral. But this work is not, as is often supposed, an attack on the *Astrée*, which Sorel sincerely admired. It is rather a protest against the precious jargon and extravagant imagery which, not only in France but in other countries, had become associated with pastoral literature. Of course, novelists like D'Urfé, Du Rosset and D'Audiguier come in for their share of knocks, but the poets of antiquity and of his own time are also severely taken to task. It is well known that Sorel detested poetry. A facile prose writer, he was incapable of producing a line of verse. He had that literal type of mind which looks on metaphor as an offence to reason, so he makes very merry with the "flinty hearts," the "complexions of lilies and roses," and the "ensnaring tresses" which his colleagues freely attributed to their heroines. To lovers of poetry the *Berger extravagant* makes no appeal, which is a pity, since apart from its exaggerations the general conception of the novel is amusing, if not quite original.

The story is briefly this. The hero Lysis is a real shepherd, a half - wit who has lost the other half through too much reading of pastoral novels. Having abandoned his law studies at the Sorbonne, he retires to the country, where, in the company of a few mangy sheep, he cultivates the simple life and waits for his Astrée. She appears under the name of Charite, a country wench and a chambermaid to boot. Thanks to the malice of certain practical jokers who promise themselves much amusement at the expense of Lysis, the situations of the *Astrée* are duplicated for the benefit of the wretched butt. Nymphs, woodland sprites, magicians and enchanted castles provide the necessary background for the activities of the bemused hero. So seriously does he enter into his rôle that on one occasion, on being informed by the bogus enchanter that he has been changed into a tree, Lysis remains in the trunk of a rotten willow, where, but for his persecutors relenting, he would have starved for his ideals. By this method of contrast, then, does Sorel try to destroy the pastoral and to make way for the novel reflecting real life. But his technique is poor. His very seriousness militates against the success of his plan. The same didactic manner which we noted in *Francion* becomes in the *Berger extravagant* the worst form of pedantry, and the author frequently falls into the error which he imputes to Cervantes, that of imitating the very weakness which he seeks to ridicule. To a large degree, though he strenuously denies it, he is dependent on *Don Quijote*, but it is possible that Lysis may have been immediately suggested by the extraordinary conduct of Monsieur des Yveteaux, a former tutor of Louis XIII. This gentleman became so enamoured of the pastoral idea that he assumed the garb of Céladon, and, complete with crook and straw hat lined with satin, this odd figure could be seen driving imaginary flocks along the avenues of his estate, singing his chansonettes and warding off phantom wolves. The *Berger extravagant* was well received and ran through fifteen editions in the seventeenth century alone.

In his *Bibliothèque française*, Sorel, in discussing *romans comiques*, mentions in this category D'Aubigné's *Les Aventures du Baron de Fœneste*, which is, however, a polemic rather than a novel, written, says the author, to distract a mind "lassé de discours graves et tragiques," and which finds recreation in presenting a satirical description of the century in the form of a dialogue. It appeared in 1617. Jean de Lannel's satirical picture of the aristocracy which he offers in his *Roman satyrique* (1623) is a confused jumble of improbability and reality without the slightest trace of talent. There is more art in the unfinished autobiographical narrative called *Le Page disgracié* (1643), by Tristan l'Hermite, in which the author, in the form of a novel, claims to give an unvarnished account of his life as page to a natural son of Henri IV. Tristan compares his work to the re-

flection of a mirror, and it is indeed a faithful picture
of the manners of various sections of polite society.
As has been frequently pointed out, it is one of the
first examples of the *mémoires* type of novel which
flourished so abundantly in the eighteenth century.

Sorel, who realised that the comic novel was too
often marred by licence, attempted to provide an
unobjectionable *histoire comique* in *Polyandre* (1648),
which, however, he never finished. In his preface he
exposes his conception of this type of novel. The true
histoire comique should be a naïve picture of the
various humours of mankind in which the author
censures human foibles by means of ridicule. Speaking
of the "ten thousand volumes of *romans*" which had
appeared in France since the beginning of the century, he complains that the only human activity
which they portray is that of making love. His intention is very clear. It is to found a novel which will
reflect the ordinary daily occupations of the average
man, and thus provide the reader with an account
of such adventures as might occur to persons of his
acquaintance — in a word, to institute a novel of
manners. Yet, apart altogether from the fact that
Polyandre is unfinished, Sorel's performance, as always,
falls short of his ambition. There is no unity in this
collection of detached descriptions and portraits. True
one finds in it occasional silhouettes of curious seventeenth-century figures and sidelights on the intimate
life of financiers and bourgeois. Still, the fidelity of
such pictures is annulled by an incorrigible tendency
to caricature. And here is precisely the weakness of

all French seventeenth-century *romans comiques*.
Sorel, Scarron, Furetière, and later even Lesage,
when they transport comedy from the stage to the
novel, fail to allow for the fact that the comic exaggeration which is essential to the optics of the theatre
produces in fiction an atmosphere of unreality and
throws the novelist's picture out of focus. It is interesting in this connection to note that Molière's
Tartuffe owes something to *Polyandre*, for his Mme
Pernelle is certainly imitated from Sorel's Mme
Ragonde, the old lady who spends her life regretting
the "good old times." It is possible, too, that many
traits of Tartuffe himself were suggested by the
episode of Polyandre disguised as the holy friar
Polycarpe.

Had Scarron done nothing else, we must yet be
grateful to him for shortening the novel. Of course,
his *Roman comique* (1651) is incomplete, since the
existing third part is from the pen of Girault. Still,
it is clear from the author's plan, communicated
verbally to friends, and from the rapidity of his
narrative, that there was no ground for apprehen-
sion on the score of prolixity. This little *cul de jatte*
who preceded a king in the enjoyment of Mme de
Maintenon's favours is one of the most human figures
in the pageant of the seventeenth century. A Figaro
ravaged by disease, he found a refuge from the ugliness of life, not like the *précieuses* by ignoring its
realities, but by cultivating the blessed gift of humour.
If Scarron did not invent the burlesque style, he
practised it with such dexterity that it has become

inextricably associated with his name. In the French novel the art of travesty had already been cultivated of course by Sorel, but not with that lightness of touch and unfailing good humour which made the fortune of the *Roman comique*.

From the point of view of human interest Scarron's choice of subject is a happy one. In every age there is something romantic and alluring about the life of the strolling actor. The novel opens with a vividly drawn picture of a travelling theatre on the road. It has been conjectured, indeed, that it is the very "Illustre Théâtre" in which Molière and Mlle Béjart toured the provinces for thirteen years. It does not matter. What interests the reader is the account of the daily adventures of this little band of nomads and social pariahs. In Scarron's pages we see the old actor trudging along bowed down beneath an enormous 'cello, for all the world, says the author, like a great turtle walking on its hind-legs. They pass the village inn, pursued by hooting children. The ponderous burghers gaze at them suspiciously and the officious provost's lieutenant rides forward importantly to ask them their business.

The players are the rallying-point towards which gravitates the society of Le Mans, the principal town in the limited circuit visited by the troupe. By circumscribing their movements in this way, Scarron makes it possible for the reader to enjoy those descriptions of provincial manners which provide a background to his more detailed picture of the actors themselves. In the interpolated stories related by Destin, the very gallant gentleman who leads the company, and by La Caverne, the eldest of the actresses, the writer creates an atmosphere of romance and imagination which offsets the crude realism and coarseness of his other manner. Ragotin, the romantic little bourgeois who leaves his small estate and follows the troupe out of love for one of the *comédiennes*, is the universal butt whose mishaps delight the groundlings. But Scarron's most original creation is undoubtedly La Rancune, the morose, elderly actor who takes a sardonic delight in silent practical jokes, sometimes of a grisly sort. He is the man born with a grievance: the Cadwallader of the French novel.

Scarron has the gift of grouping his characters, an effective trick which betrays the playwright in him. He has also the comic author's art of producing the illusion of movement. Indeed, some of his situations, with very little alteration, could be transported on the stage—for example, the famous scene where little Ragotin finds his view of the stage interrupted by the enormous back of a stolid bourgeois. His excited invitations to "sit down" are persistently ignored, since the fat man is already seated. The *dénouement* with its *coups de poing* and general uproar is in the best Tabarin manner, and the curtain falls on the struggling Ragotin, who has been pushed into the theatre cess-pit. Scarron describes the life of the troupe with great fidelity. He tells us of their organisation, their discipline, their rites, their repertoire, their jealousies, and their amazing esprit de corps. All receipts are pooled and all decisions arrived at in conference. The author evokes a company of hard-working artistes fond of good cheer but not debauched. They are intelligent and understand the plays they interpret, since the majority have enjoyed a good upbringing. And this conception of Scarron's is after all an extremely plausible one, when we reflect that the greater part of the revenues of such companies was derived from the generosity of cultured gentlemen at whose houses they were often in demand.

The author greatly admired the Spanish *nouvelles* or short stories, which he claimed were more palatable to the average reader than the pseudo-classic novel of the Scudéry type. He imitated several of these in the tales which he intercalated in the *Roman comique*. It is clear, too, that he relished the picaresque novel, the heroes of which furnished suggestions for his swaggering, venal La Rappinière.

The *Roman comique* is from every point of view a protest against the improbability and exaggeration of contemporary romantic fiction. It ridicules the painstaking descriptions of novels like *Polexandre*, *Bassa*, and *Cyrus*, "the most completely furnished novel in the world," says Scarron ironically. He himself, however, did not despise detail, but with him such picturesque and minute description is reserved for persons and actions, and not for *milieu*. A master of the ironic lapidary phrase, he is suggestive to a high degree. Thus to describe an inn at night: "Le silence régnait dans l'hostellerie; les chiens y dormaient puisqu'ils n'aboyaient point." Ragotin in the throes of love is described as "pressé de son amour

comme d'un mal de ventre." The priest officiating
at the funeral of a miser: "le curé fit des prières sur
le mort et les fit bonnes car il les fit courtes." And to
show the attitude of the bourgeois towards the man
of letters: "ils reprocheraient à un homme qu'il
fait des livres comme ils lui reprocheraient qu'il *fait
de la fausse monnaie.*" Readers of *Gil Blas* will notice
something of Lesage's manner, but there is no universal picture of *mœurs* in the *Roman comique* which,
though an excellent reflection of manners, is deliberately restricted to that field with which the author
is familiar. However, this novel is one of the most
realistic works of the seventeenth century. Its defects
are those peculiar to this particular stage of the
development of the French novel in general, lack of
unity of interest and of course absence of psychology
in character-portrayal.

Notwithstanding the enormous popularity of the
individual *histoires comiques* which we have cited,
it must be admitted that the evolution of this sort
of novel proceeded very slowly. The explanation is
easy to discover. The elements which compose works
of this kind are those which we find in comedy—
farce, pictures of manners and satire. Again, many
of their characters are *caractères*, that is, composite
personages which embody the attributes we associate with a particular foible or vice. It is not
surprising, then, that, in view of the immense success
of Molière and his school, the comic and realistic
novel of manners should have been overshadowed
by comedy. As we shall see, the history of the de-

velopment of the novel provides many illustrations
of this phenomenon. A period of florescence in one
type of literature frequently synchronises with a
period of depression in another. One cannot, however, go so far as to use the word "law" in this connection, since it sometimes happens that in a genre
which has sunk into a listless condition there arises
a writer who by sheer genius compels attention. It
is, further, not always the case that such apparitions
are followed by a general renaissance of the type of
literature affected, for those very qualities of individuality and originality which were responsible for
their fame often tend to discourage imitation.

There is also another explanation of the tardy development of the *histoire comique*, but as it is bound
up with the origins of another current of the novel
it may be postponed till we have examined Furetière's
Roman bourgeois, which continues the line of the comic
novel of manners.

The first part of the *Roman bourgeois* has the form
of a novel; the second, as the author informs us in
his preface, is merely a collection of disjointed "petites
histoires et aventures arrivées en divers quartiers de
la ville." This second book consists in fact of a rather
wearisome satire on Charles Sorel (Charroselles), together with a relation of the oddities of two eccentrics,
Belastre, an impossibly stupid magistrate famous for
his malapropisms, and Collantine, a woman with a
mania for litigation. To return to the first book, we
discover here a certain unity. There are two inter-
woven plots dealing with the love affairs of Lucrèce,

a coquettish bourgeoise, the victim of an indiscreet admiration for the nobility, and of Javotte, the ingenuous daughter of Vollichon, a rascally *procureur*. But all the interest lies in Furetière's excellent sketch of Parisian manners. He avoids the exuberance of Scarron, and by concentrating on character-portrayal admirably reflects the intimate life of that section of the middle classes engaged in the less important branches of the law. The author was born in Paris and had first-hand knowledge of his subject, since he was for a time a counsel at the Parlement and later procurator-fiscal at Saint-Germain des Prés. The chicanery of the profession is well known to him, the art of prolonging a profitable case by procuring the intervention of new parties, the perfidious system by which a lawyer draws up a deed for nothing and charges double the usual fee for registration, in fact the Dodson-and-Fogg end of the business. The clannishness of the profession is well illustrated in the matter of Javotte's marriage, for all the suitors are from the Palais de Justice.

Furetière detests the section of the bourgeoisie which apes the gentry. He ridicules these *précieuses*, and significantly attributes the disorganisation of the Vollichon household to the romantic ideas which Javotte acquires at one of their *salons*. Lucrèce's seduction by a nobleman who offers marriage and meanly abstracts his written promise is yet another warning against the folly of going outside one's station. He understands the bourgeois mind to a nicety. Avarice, industry and caution are the characteristics of the middle class. Marriage is a complicated affair in which love plays little part. "Nicomède took counsel of his friends and not of his love, which disappeared shortly afterwards; for love is not so obstinate in the head of a bourgeois as it is in the heart of a hero. Engagements are lightly entered upon and as easily broken. Interest and the desire to settle down are what regulate their passion. It is only idlers and novel heroes whose fidelity is proof against hardship, absence and the years." Such is Furetière's outlook on life: the outlook of the disillusioned realist. The novel is for him a document, "a very true and sincere narrative." The *Roman bourgeois* is in this respect a precocious work and a precursor of the realistic fiction of the nineteenth century.

CHAPTER III

WE have just witnessed the beginnings of a conscious effort to introduce probability into the French novel. The modern critic is now so accustomed to look upon verisimilitude as a *sine qua non* of prose fiction, that he is prone to under-estimate the difficulties and the achievement of these early seventeenth-century novelists. The critic of that time, when he troubles to recognise the existence of fiction as an independent genre, and that is but seldom, conceives the novel purely as a sort of prose epic. The historical importance of Sorel and his followers lies in the fact that they helped to break down this narrow conception by revealing the possibility of a novel which, whilst retaining the charm of poetry in the most literal sense of the word, might yet dispense with the supernatural motivation and improbable adventures which had become associated with the pastoral and heroic novel. What were probably the views of the average critic of 1679 on this question are reflected in an unpublished article written on that date by Pierre Perrault, one of three gifted brothers famous in literary history. Novels, he says, may be roughly divided into two classes—poetic and

comic; though indeed they are all poetic in the sense
that they are all fictions. The first category embraces
works of prose fiction which present the adventures
of great princes and the love affairs of illustrious
"bergers." On account of their style, which is highly
ornamental, such novels are known as *poèmes*, and
by virtue of this title their authors are allowed to
indulge in all sorts of improbabilities, though indeed
the use of the supernatural is now scarcely tolerated.
The comic novel, on the other hand, excludes everything which is not natural and which does not conform to ordinary life. These two manners, observes
Perrault, correspond to the two schools of painting
then in vogue, the conventional and naturalistic; an
excellent analogy if one contrasts, for instance, the
manner of a Poussin with that of a Le Nain.

The defect of the *histoire comique* in the eyes of
contemporaries was its failure to respect the social
and literary prejudices of the century. In an aristocratic age which insisted upon the moral and æsthetic
purpose of its literature, even the comic genius of a
Molière failed to placate the austerity of Bossuet and
Fénelon. The realism of Scarron and his colleagues
was tolerated as a necessary adjunct to satire, but
it was only tolerated. Plainly the salvation of the
novel did not lie in that direction. Sorel was aware
of this fact when, in 1623, he produced his *Nouvelles
françaises*, in which he abandoned realism for romantic
probability. And it is clear from his reminiscences
that he regretted the offence against good taste of
which he was guilty in his *Francion* and *Berger*

extravagant. Confronted with the necessity of choosing between two currents each of which seemed likely to lead to the desired goal, Sorel hesitated and compromised. Both in his imitation of the foreign *nouvelle* and in his attempt to found a national and popular novel of manners, this writer did much to bring the French novel closer to real life, yet failed to evolve a type of fiction which should give rise to a school.

Segrais, although less productive than Sorel as a novelist, anticipated him as a theorist. The preface to his *Divertissements de la Princesse Aurélie* (1656) is a most suggestive document. Like the author of *Francion,* Segrais attacks the idealistic novel of his time, in this case the heroic novel as popularised by Scudéry. Less violent than Sorel, he realises the good qualities of these heroic productions, though keenly alive to their limitations. The art of the novelist is to entertain by means of "probable and natural fictions." He sees no reason why the novel should not be instructive, particularly if the author is well informed as to the history and manners of the foreign nations which he describes. Here Segrais lays bare what was at once the strength and weakness of the heroic novel: its historical setting. Incidentally he reveals also one of the factors which discredited the novel generally in the eyes of the critic. "To tell the truth," he says, referring to certain novelists of the Scudéry school, "the great liberties which some have taken with historical truth, those facile interviews and those long conversations which they attribute in *ruelles* to men and women from countries where facilities for intercourse are not so great as in France, and the purely French manners which they impute to Greeks, Persians and Indians are things which are far from reasonable." Here we have an interesting point of difference between tragedy and the novel. The enthusiastic crowds who flocked to see the plays of Racine accepted the pseudo-classic setting as a mere convention, but in their fiction apparently they desired greater probability. The explanation of this seeming anomaly is possibly this. In tragedy the cadre is necessarily unobtrusive: the main interest lies in the spectacle of the conflict of wills or in the triumph of character over circumstances. Here the important matter is psychological truth, and that is precisely the essence of Racinian tragedy. Pending the appearance of a psychological novel modelled on tragedy, the French were accustomed to expect in their fiction a reflection of the manners and an echo of the conversation of fashionable society, relieved by fascinating though improbable historical and geographical descriptions. The first reform suggested by Segrais, then, is directed at the cadre and not at the essence of the novel. It is external, not internal.

His procedure is extremely logical. He first proposes to substitute for the improbable Parthians and Scythians of the heroic novel French knights or princes. Here he realises one of the foibles of the French reader, who finds something more romantic or exotic in an Artabize or an Orosmane than in plain Rohan or Montmorency. Yet, he argues, the Spaniards give only national names to their characters and

localities. Warming to his thesis, he suggests that
the novel would still be more interesting if, instead
of presenting the enterprises of kings and emperors,
it were to choose its heroes from some less inaccessible
section of society.

But Segrais' most practical achievement was to
discard the *roman* for the *nouvelle*, and by so doing
he performed an inestimable service, shortening
the French novel and making it a probable reflection of life. That he did so deliberately is clear
from his own words. "We have undertaken to narrate
things as they are, not as they should be. Besides,
it seems to me that here is the difference between
the *roman* and the *nouvelle*. The former describes
things conventionally and poetically: the latter should
partake rather of history and confine itself prefer-
ably to giving images of things as we usually see
them, and not as our imagination pictures them." It
is regrettable that Segrais' performance falls so far
short of his intention. The short stories which compose the *Divertissements* conform only superficially to
his plan, and apart from their national and historical
dress they display many of the improbabilities of the
long heroic novel, the disguises, recognitions and extraordinary adventures which persist so long in French
fiction. Still, it would be ungrateful to withhold from
Segrais his meed of praise or to judge his work by
what was after all his maiden effort.

In 1664 the indefatigable Sorel, commenting on
the publication of a *nouvelle* called *La Princesse de
Montpensier*, observes that it is the work of "une

personne de haute condition et d'excellent esprit qui
se contente de faire de belles choses sans que son nom
soit publié." If we believe the gossip of the day, the
adventures of this story were real and contemporary,
though the actors were disguised. The "personne de
haute condition" is of course Mme de Lafayette, the
intimate friend of La Rochefoucauld and also of
Segrais, who collaborated with her, though to what
extent can only be conjectured. The generally accepted opinion is that the *Princesse de Montpensier*,
Zaïde, and the very short novelette *La Comtesse de
Tende*, show evidence of Segrais' hand. The masterpiece known as *La Princesse de Clèves* was, however,
most probably the result of the daily conversations
between Mme de Lafayette and La Rochefoucauld,
the brilliant pessimist whose *Maximes* take their place
amongst the classics of French literature. The point is
one of purely academic interest: it is the tendencies
displayed in the novels which touch us here.

The decade 1662 to 1672 is an interesting one in
the history of the evolution of the French novel.
Corneille, his best work accomplished, had come to
Paris. The star of Racine's genius waxed bright, and
Molière's mighty laughter re-echoed through a land
which, if it but knew, had very little to laugh at.
In 1665 Boileau was reading the manuscript of his
Dialogue sur les Héros de Roman before a chosen
circle, and making a great to-do about his gentle-
manliness in postponing the publication of the satire
till after the death of Mlle de Scudéry. However, as
we gather from Ménage, about this very time the

authoress of *Clélie*, realising perfectly that the heroic
sort of novel was already out of favour, refrained from
publishing her latest effort in this vein knowing well
that no one would buy it. It is worth while noting the
fact, since critics persist in attributing the decline of
the heroic novel to the influence of Boileau's satire,
which was not printed till 1710, a classic instance of
"post hoc, ergo propter hoc." Society had never been
more brilliant. At Versailles love and gallantry reigned
supreme and, fortified by the example of a young and
full-blooded monarch, the court played havoc with
the ten commandments pending the chill and ghostly
apparition of Mme de Maintenon.

Mlle Lavergne, or Mme de Lafayette as she became after marriage, was twenty when she began
to write her novels on married life. To begin with,
here was a decided innovation, a novel starting off at
the point to which the old *roman héroïque* attained
only after endless vicissitudes and an unconscion-
able expenditure of ink. The precious heroine of the
idealistic story, with her intolerable *sainte-nitouche*
mannerisms, makes way for a creature of flesh and
blood capable of inspiring and feeling passion. Tragic
love, unknown in the French novel since the sixteenth
century, reappears in the form originally popularised
in France by Boccaccio and Cervantes, that of the
nouvelle. But meanwhile other and greater influences
have been at work, for there is in *La Princesse
de Montpensier*, as in all Mme de Lafayette's work,
much more than the narrative of a guilty love adventure. Where her individuality is most sharply em-

phasised is in the moral purpose which reveals itself in all her novels, and it is here that we observe the line of cleavage between the French and foreign schools. La princesse de Montpensier is married to a man who deceives her. She struggles for a time against her passion for the duc de Guise. Her husband's best friend, Chabannes, is also in love with her, but hopelessly. To keep at least her friendship, he acts as an intermediary between Mme de Montpensier and the duc de Guise. Inevitably the husband stumbles on a rendezvous, and Chabannes saves the situation in so far as is possible by aiding Guise to escape and by allowing his friend the prince to think him guilty. The *dénouement* is tragic. Chabannes is massacred in Paris, whither he fled on Saint Bartholomew's Eve, and the princess, having lost a perfect friend, a husband's respect and the love of the faithless Guise, dies of grief. I use the word *dénouement* purposely, because the structure of this novel is that of French classic tragedy. The choice of a definite theme, the ability to expose a situation and to conduct it to a logical climax, and above all the art of portraying the gradual disintegration of the will under the corrosive influence of a grand passion — these were new elements in the novel which now, in imitation of tragedy, attempts something greater than mere fidelity in the reproduction of external detail. Led by Mme de Lafayette, the novelist strives to give a probable picture of the sentiments and passions, and later to disclose the hidden springs which motivate human conduct. The psychological novel is born.

Zaïde (1670) is frankly disappointing. Segrais has of course been blamed for the banal adventures and improbabilities reminiscent of Scudéry. There are, however, purple patches, and these have naturally been ascribed to Mme de Lafayette. Undoubtedly the outstanding episode is the intercalated story of Alphonse and Bélisare, a little masterpiece of psychological portraiture. Briefly it is the analysis of the soul of a lover who tortures himself by listening to the account of the love affairs of his mistress. Bélisare has been loved often, but Alphonse is the first to touch a responsive chord in her heart. Hopelessly she resists his unreasonable request for a "confession," knowing well that it must be the end of their love. Here again the *dénouement* is tragic, for the mutual friend of the lovers falls a victim to Alphonse's insane jealousy.

The story of *La Princesse de Clèves* is almost too well known to need repetition. This classic represents the highest degree of perfection attained by the French novel prior to the Romantic period, with perhaps the one exception of Prévost's *Manon Lescaut*. It is a perfect tragedy in the form of the novel, and very simply told in the restrained manner of the time. A wife confesses to her husband that she is in love with another man. Her husband, whom she respects but does not love, sympathises with her and esteems her for her frankness. The other man is a philanderer and, as it transpires, is unworthy of a great love. The real drama lies in the effort of the husband and wife to dominate, on the one hand jealousy, and on the other passion. There is no need to look far afield for the model, for here we have an example of one of the best qualities of Corneillian tragedy, the triumph of the will over circumstances. But, in the delicate nuances composing that magnificent psychological study which is presented by the character of Mme de Clèves, it is to Racine and not to Corneille that we must turn if we seek comparisons. The ending is relentlessly logical. The prince de Clèves, imagining that his wife has yielded to temptation, dies, but not before hearing the truth. His death purifies his wife's heart of every vestige of passion for her lover, and she is able to face him unshaken in her resolve to expiate her sin in a convent. The nobility of the confession scene aroused the admiration of contemporaries like Fontenelle, though there were many who found it improbable and quixotic. D'Haussonville, a nineteenth-century critic, called it a literary discovery, and indeed it is. Yet what is the conduct of the prince de Clèves but the inevitable apotheosis of the feminine cult as practised by the hero of the idealist school of novelists; only, thanks to the genius of Mme de Lafayette, what in the heroic novel would have been another of those innumerable and wearisome cases of conscience has been transmuted into an intensely human and dramatic situation. The virtue of abnegation, which is essentially the triumph of will over passion, becomes henceforth a favourite subject with French writers, and it is obvious that sensibility originates in the novel with the advent of *La Princesse de*

Clèves. Segrais, and it is but fair to mention this, raised the question in one of his *nouvelles.* "Can a lover honourably give up his mistress to a rival?" But it was Mme de Lafayette who exploited the dramatic possibilities of such a theme in her *Princesse de Montpensier* and in *Zaïde,* and in the *Princesse de Clèves.*

The more interesting problem of whether a woman should confess to her husband her love for another man may have been suggested by memories of *Polyeucte.* This view has been much canvassed, but I cannot subscribe to it. The authoress herself indeed stresses the originality of her conception. As to its merit, few will agree with Bussy-Rabutin that it is "extravagant," but with Fontenelle most readers will regret that the lover M. de Nemours is made to overhear the conversation between the husband and wife. Fontenelle's criticism is unfortunately true: "Cela sent un peu l'*Astrée.*" Still, that is a minor point which detracts not at all from the grandeur of the main theme. The conception of a husband who realises that he no longer possesses his wife's love, nay, that he never possessed it, and yet who is neither a fool nor something worse, was revolutionary in 1678. The conflict between reason and passion, between generosity and jealousy, did not appeal to some of Mme de Lafayette's contemporaries, though, like all great novels, this one provided food for interesting speculation, and, because it is a classic, continues to do so. Is confession, to any other than a priest, a needless cruelty, notwithstanding the worthiness of the sentiment which actuates it? Bélisare and Mme de Clèves indirectly cause the deaths of two innocent men. In the case of the latter, the confession is spontaneous and due to the consciousness that her will alone is not strong enough to withstand temptation. One critic, M. d'Haussonville, points to the interesting fact that nowhere does Mme de Clèves invoke spiritual aid, and comments admiringly on her stoic detachment, her *virtus*. But surely the logical conclusion which the attentive reader will arrive at is that here, as in all Mme de Lafayette's works, the moral is that the Church alone is capable of giving solace and disinterested advice, and alone worthy to receive confession. Although our knowledge of the relations of La Rochefoucauld and Mme de Lafayette is very meagre, this has not deterred some writers from seeking in the latter's work those personal applications which the heroic and romantic schools of novelists have accustomed us to expect. I fear that in the case of Mme de Lafayette such conjectures carry little conviction, because of their lack of any real basis of fact.

It has been left to a German writer, Herr Waldburg, to apply the methods of a questionable school of modern psychology to the criticism of *La Princesse de Clèves*. He speaks of her "moral adultery," thus imputing to the authoress intentions which she certainly never possessed, for Mme de Clèves is described as innocent both as to conduct and intent. If she were guilty of concupiscence her confession to her husband would be an impudent lie, a conception which would have shocked the reader as much as it would have astonished the authoress herself. The contemporaries of Mme de Lafayette, as we have seen, attacked her book only on the score of improbability: the subconscious motives of the authoress disturbed them not at all. The *Comtesse de Tende* is a reply to current reproaches touching the improbability of the confession scene. Here the heroine is actually guilty of adultery, the results of which can no longer be concealed. Her lover is killed and she confesses to her husband. Pending the consequences of his fury, the countess dies in an agony of remorse, a banal treatment of a banal situation, and one which serves merely to throw into stronger relief the artistic beauty and originality of the *Princesse de Clèves*.

It must not be forgotten that Mme de Lafayette was an historian of some repute. It is possible to overlook this fact when one examines the cadre of her novels, since with her the historical background is extremely vague, a mere excuse indeed to situate her characters in appropriate surroundings. The names are, of course, well known in French history, but there is no effort to conform to fact in the description of the personages. The manners and adventures set forth are those of the reign of Louis XIV., but in deference to what the seventeenth century called *bienséance*, that scrupulous regard for the feelings of contemporaries which has now unhappily disappeared from literature, the authoress deliberately ante-dated her scenes to the period of Henri II. and Charles IX. The novelist, ever on the look out for accessories which might enhance that

illusion of truth called probability, passed from
Utopia to the Ancient World, and thence to the
national *milieu*, in obedience to the growing public
demand for verisimilitude. In this aspect of its
evolution, the novel moved more swiftly than the
sister genre of tragedy, since it is not until the
eighteenth century that we find any attempt to
reform the impossible costume and setting of
dramatic productions. But there is another reason.
The novel is an acquisitive and imitative type of
literature. We have seen that it does not scruple to
extract from tragedy the essential qualities of psychological veracity and logical structure. It is but
natural that history, which resembles the novel
more closely than any other form of literature,
should also pay tribute to the invader, and one of
the most frequent claims of seventeenth-century
novelists is a respect for chronology. Thanks largely
to the influence of Segrais, the imitation or pre-
tended imitation of history becomes more and more
evident. The old title *histoire* no longer stands alone.
Mémoires, *Histoires secrètes* and *Relations* begin to
appear on the title-pages of highly imaginative fictions, and the example of Mme de Lafayette leads
to a general pillage of historical treatises, which
are ransacked for material. A flourishing school of
popular novelists, mostly women, flooded the book-
shops with sentimental and tragic novels, the majority
of which, like *La Princesse de Clèves*, borrowed their
setting from French or English history. For the love
theme, however, which forms the chief attraction

of such publications, the authors resorted to their own fertile imaginations and to a natural gift for observation.

Before attempting to explore the chief tendencies of this school, let us glance for a moment at one or two productions which are not without interest, though they lie somewhat off the path we are immediately following. On all sides there are signs in literature of a general movement towards probability, a chafing against the unwritten code which controls the literary expression of personal emotions and ideas. The novel, as we have seen, moves closer to life and becomes more spontaneous. Without warning, however, there appeared in 1668 a tiny volume called *Les Lettres d'une Religieuse portugaise*, which astonished and delighted a society that had raised the writing of letters to an art. The author of these seven letters was unknown, but in the usual mysterious preface it was given out that they were the work of a Portuguese nun, who had been seduced and deserted by a French officer serving in Portugal. After a century of conjecture, it seemed in 1810 that the mystery was at last solved. An erudite bibliophile discovered on the fly-leaf of his copy of the letters a note giving the name of the unhappy nun as Marianne Alcaforado, and that of the officer as the maréchal de Chamilly. The letters were said to have been translated by a certain Guilleraques. Later research appeared to corroborate these statements, though a few critics still remained sceptical. By accident, the writer of this study recently stumbled upon the *privilège* granted to the publisher of the letters, which plainly states that they were written by one Guilleraques, and so are not authentic after all. It is of course regrettable that so many precious tears have been wasted over the unhappy Marianne, who thus stands convicted, with Diderot's *Religieuse*, of having obtained sympathy under false pretences. But on one point no controversy is possible. All Europe agrees as to the artistic perfection of these pathetic letters, which are quick with the misery of a woman who lost all for love. The moment of their appearance was propitious. The reaction against formalism, in the expression of the emotions, as evidenced for example in *La princesse de Montpensier*, was revealing itself also in the restrained ardour of Racine and Pascal. Still, so powerful is the force of tradition in French literature, that it is doubtful if the unconventional and personal tone of the *Lettres portugaises* would have been tolerated without the fiction contained in the preface. That very conservatism which makes the French so critical of their own writers, usually carries with it a tolerance for the emotional indiscretions of other nations which is a source of perpetual wonder to the foreigner. Undoubtedly these *Lettres* influenced the French novel, where they encouraged an already growing trend in the direction of sentiment, besides doing much to establish the foundations of the epistolary novel. Do not let us, however, like so many critics, over-estimate this influence, which is best regarded as one of several contributory causes to the gradual unshackling of

sentiment in the French novel. It is as well not to
forget, either, that much of the admiration aroused
by the *Lettres portugaises* had in it a fair share of
that enthusiasm which a literary phenomenon always
produces in curious and intelligent minds.

The appearance of the first French literary journal,
in 1672, helped indirectly to increase the popularity
of the *nouvelle*. *Le Mercure galant*, which ran from
1672 till 1674, contains some remarkably good short
stories, whose authors add their quota to the criticism
then being directed against the heroic novel. Subligny,
in his *Fausse Clélie* (1670), attacks the cult for pseudo-
classicism and claims the honour of first introducing French names into the novel. "I am a good
Picardian," he boasts, "who calls every man by his
proper name." It is interesting, also, to note that
in his *Folle Querelle ou critique d'Andromaque* (1668)
he does not scruple to make fun of Racine, whose
Pyrrhus, he claims, must have read *Clélie*. Here we
may safely accord him the honours of priority, since
not even the punctilious Boileau could detect any
flaw in the writings of his friend. It is not inappro-
priate to mention at this stage the *Mémoires de la
Vie de Henriette Sylvie de Molière* (1674), which were
long ascribed to Subligny, though most probably they
came from the fertile pen of Mme de Villedieu. This
novel is written in autobiographical form and, despite
the intricacies of its plot, still makes good reading,
since it is a picture of the manners of high society,
and contains also amusing sallies against the conventional hero of the long-winded Scudéry school. Mme

de Villedieu, whose life was more romantic than any
of her novels, is the first of that long line of prolific
novelists whose works now lie undisturbed in the
dusty fastnesses of the Bibliothèque Nationale. Un-
distinguished as to style, and carelessly thrown
together, these novels affect, for the most part, the
form of *mémoires*. They reflect the daily life of the
polite society of their day, but their chief concern
is amorous adventure. Some of these fictions are
doubtless romanced versions of actual contemporary
scandals, and indeed some of the most improbable
of their adventures are really founded on fact. They
have not survived because they are topical, and also
because they contain no measure of that universal
truth which alone imparts immortality to a novel.
On the other hand, one cannot ignore these straws
which betray the direction of the currents and eddies
of the novel. Without a knowledge of such lesser
novels of the seventeenth and eighteenth centuries,
the great figures like Lesage, Marivaux and Prévost
must appear like sudden apparitions arising out of
the void, and not, as they really are, the natural
products of their literary and social surroundings.
Much of the work of great novelists will always
remain inexplicable, that is to say the part which
we vaguely attribute to genius: there remains, however, another element, which is derived from the
influence of predecessors and contemporaries, for in
literature, as in the sciences, absolute originality does
not exist. "On est toujours de son siècle."
  In her *Annales galantes* (1670), Mme de Villedieu

takes her place along with the great number of women novelists of the Lafayette school. The sentimental novels of this type, whose love adventures were enacted in an historical, usually court setting, were amazingly popular and apparently lucrative, for Quincye de Saint-Maurice tells us that Mme de Villedieu received a hundred sous a page from Barbin the publisher, who, if we believe Lesage, was not given to throwing money away. Exalted ladies like the comtesse de Murat did not scorn to contribute to the rapidly swelling list of historical novels. Her *Comte de Dunois* (1671) is ingeniously constructed and still readable. Mlle de Rocheguilhen levied toll on the histories of Spain, Portugal and England, and her *Comte d'Essex* and her *Anne de Boulen* pandered to the taste of a large body of readers who confidently believed that they were combining entertainment with instruction. One of the most sentimental writers of this school was undoubtedly Catherine Bernard, whose *Malheurs de l'Amour* (1687) glorifies the virtue of renunciation in love. Eleanor, the heroine, gives up her suitor, the duc de Mesnil, to her rival Mathilde, and marries another man with whom she lived "as one whose virtue was perfect, though ever unhappy because of the passion she cherished in her heart." Mlle Bernard deliberately chose exceptional situations, as for example in the *Comte d'Amboise* (1689), where the hero gives up his mistress to a rival. The authoress naïvely remarks that the action is uncommon, and therefore improbable. She appeals, however, to a select company of readers large-minded enough to

waive the question of improbability, in view of the
nobility of the central idea. It is only just to agree
with Bernard that, in depicting the sentiments, she
has tried "to differentiate between a real passion
and the rational idea of a passion."

Whilst in most of these novels little attention is
paid to historical accuracy, an exception must be
made for Mlle Caumont de la Force. Inaccurate as
to facts, she does at least try to make her characters conform to accepted tradition, and her *Histoire
secrète de Bourgogne* (1694) preserves at least the
illusion of history. After all, as an eighteenth-century
commentator remarked: "So many historians have
given us romance in place of history, that we must
not judge too severely the novels of Mlle de la Force,
which have not that pretension." This authoress,
exploiting Mlle Bernard's favourite renunciation *motif*,
carries on the new tradition of respect for psychological truth in the analysis of the sentiments. Another
popular transition novelist, the comtesse d'Aulnoy,
in her *Comte de Warwick* (1703), tried to break away
from the tragic manner which had become associated
with the sentimental and historical novel, and though,
as usual, the foreign setting is merely a disguise for
contemporary adventures, there is a slight attempt
to reproduce the local colour of London in 1456. Mlle
Durand, Mme de Lussan and Mlle L'Héritier, to cite
only three names from the copious list of writers
belonging to this sentimental feminist group, carry
the movement into the eighteenth century, but add
little to the tendencies we have indicated.

A novelist whose initiative has not received the mention which it deserves is De Préschac, the son of a Béarnais peasant, who kept the duc d'Orléans informed as to the escapades of Parisian society. It is he, and not Mme de Villedieu, who was responsible for the *Illustre Parisienne* (1679), in which he wilfully breaks with custom and chooses as his heroine the daughter of a banker in the rue Saint-Denis, an audacious innovation for the time. There is no attempt to introduce history into this sentimental bourgeois story, which is an effort to portray middle-class life in a probable fashion and without the slightest tendency towards satire. The eighteenth-century compiler of a MS. catalogue of old novels classes as *romans d'amour bourgeois* two anonymous works called *L'Illustre Mousquetaire* (1697) and *L'Amant de bonne foi* (1672). Préschac's *Illustre Parisienne* belongs to the same category. Novels of this type were not numerous in the late seventeenth century, but under Louis XV. their number increased gradually, though it was not till the end of the eighteenth century that these "domestic" stories could be said to constitute one of the main tendencies of the novel. It is, however, interesting to note thus early in the evolution of prose fiction an effort to find a middle way between the extremes of tragedy and satirical farce, and so to break down the barriers erected between the various literary genres, and which in society separated the classes and conditions. In this respect the novelist anticipates the playwright, for it is not till the forties of the eighteenth century that we distinguish the beginnings of such a movement in the theatre.

Préschac, like many novelists whose technique and style condemn them to mediocrity, possessed a remarkably fertile imagination. His novels are cosmopolitan and topical. *Le beau Polonais* (1682) is a tale of love and adventure which echoes the stirring times when Sobieski was King of Poland. As in all Préschac's works, the chief interest is in the plot, which derives its impetus from the inevitable misunderstandings, changed letters and disguises so dear to the historical novel. His *Duchesse de Milan* (1682) is excellently written. The characters of Bonnivel Sforza and Prosper Colonna are well drawn, and Préschac creates an atmosphere of jealousy and political intrigue admirably adapted to the subject. Indeed, if we make allowances for the obvious limitations of the author, there yet remains a resemblance between the *Duchesse de Milan* and Stendhal's *Chartreuse de Parme*, which is not entirely to be explained away by a superficial similarity in the choice of theme.

CHAPTER IV

THE BIOGRAPHICAL NOVEL

As early as 1664 Sorel indicated the appearance of a new type of novel, "le récit naturel des aventures modernes comme on en met dans les histoires qu'on veut faire passer pour vraies, non seulement pour vraisemblables." We have seen already, even in the pastoral and heroic novels, a tendency to introduce references to contemporary history. Such allusions were, however, sparingly employed, and always in a veiled fashion. The sentimental court *nouvelle*, popularised by Mme de Lafayette, made use of a national cadre which was drawn, however, from a period so discreetly ante-dated as to run no risk of giving offence. Sorel, whilst by no means discouraging the novelist who seeks his material in contemporary or very recent happenings, sounds a note of warning. Taking as an example an incident related in *L'Histoire de Lysandre et de Caliste* (1615), which contains a description of a fight alleged to have taken place between two jealous women in the Place Royale in the presence of Henri IV., he remarks: "Il ne fait pas bon mentir en des choses si récentes." The inference is the very sound one that the invention of the novelist in such cases is subject to control. The choice of an historical theme automatically narrows the rôle played by the imagination and exposes the author to that most ruthless of critics, the reader who is familiar with the adventures narrated. Probability in fiction is largely a matter of popular instruction. The public is willing to be deceived, of course, but only within reasonable limits, and these limits are largely defined by the extent of its knowledge. There is, however, another aspect to this situation. The same public, critical in matters of fact, is equally eager to welcome corroboration of its own conceptions. The repetition in familiar narrative form of events already known through the medium of the duller and more serious historical treatise, far from wearying the informed reader, adds to his enjoyment the thrill of intelligent participation. The novelists referred to by Sorel were trying to meet this demand by introducing topical allusions and "modern adventures" into their fictions.

Yet one element was lacking in all such narratives. The novelist, like the historian, assumed the rôle of reporter, *relating* what the various characters said and did. With the appearance of the *récit personnel* or personal narrative, in which the hero recounts his own adventures, the French novel gained immeasurably in vividness and in probability. The *Mémoires de la Vie de Henriette Sylvie de Molière* have been alluded to as one of the earliest examples of the autobiographical type of narrative, autobiographical obviously only in form, since we are as yet far distant from the Romantic novel where author and hero become identical. Préschac adopted the form of the *récit personnel* in his *Fameux Voyageur* (1682), and doubtless so did many others.

Now, absurd as were the fantastic adventures, the battles and carousals which stuffed the heroic novels, their passing left a distinct void which was not entirely filled by the sentimental, historical novel. On the other hand, the sombre theme of the latter type of novel did not allow of the introduction of those elements which make up the lighter side of life. True, Scarron and Furetière, in their satiric novels of manners, delighted large numbers of readers with their Gallic verve, although their caricature frequently bordered on the fantastic. There was ample room, it will be seen, for a broader type of fiction, a novel of adventures reflecting also the manners of society at large, a story combining in the recital of the hero's life gallant adventure, comedy and possibly, to some extent, pathos. In the life of M. D'Artagnan, "Capitaine-Lieutenant de la Ière compagnie des Mousquetaires du Roi," a writer called Courtilz de Sandras found such elements ready to hand, and, where history was deficient, his own fertile imagination supplied the want.

An eighteenth-century bibliographer, Boudot, once defined novels as "fictions de choses qui ont pu être et qui n'ont point été," and it is precisely the apocryphal element in Sandras' *Mémoires* which justifies their inclusion in this history of the development of the novel. For Courtilz is the father of a long line of novelists whose works are the terror of the conscientious or, as he is now styled, the scientific historian. It is not that the author of the life of D'Artagnan wilfully distorts historical events. On the contrary, his accounts of battles, sieges and treaties tally in the main with the relations produced by professional chroniclers. But with what art does he vivify the dry facts of history, transforming an otherwise jejune account of dates and names into a colourful and human document! This book is more than a history: it is the story of a life. Against the changing background of political intrigue and military activity stands D'Artagnan, the resourceful, swash-buckling, amorous and gallant Béarnais. Penniless, like hundreds of other *hobereaux*, he arrives at court from his little provincial town with a sorry nag, ten crowns in his pocket, and his father's parting injunc-tions to play the man. A poor equipment for a lad of eighteen at grips with life, one might think, but add to this patrimony a sword, ever ettling to leap from its scabbard, a ready wit and a solid fund of Latin realism, and we have a hero whose worst enemies are himself, the devil and Cardinal Mazarin.

Courtilz has no defined plan. He is a raconteur who passes with dazzling rapidity from one incident to another. His *Mémoires d'Artagnan* have all the unexpectedness of life itself, yet somehow the finished novel produces that impression of coherence and completeness which is to be found in every well-told story of a career. D'Artagnan is the novel hero of an age whose novelists have yet to learn the dramatist's trick of portraying a character who by sheer force of

will overrides circumstances. Like Gil Blas, Courtilz's
musketeer accepts the kicks and ha'pence of life,
adapting himself where possible to his *milieu*, and,
where the situation is beyond his control, slipping
away gracefully with more or less damage to his
amour-propre. His attitude towards women is traditional. Grateful for past favours, he rarely lingers,
fleeing matrimony as he would a plague.

But there is more than the history of an officer's
amours in these pages, for the figure of Mazarin raises
the novel to a higher plane than that. "Son Emi-
nence!" Soon the reader learns to look forward to
these words, since always they are the prelude to
another of those long exciting struggles between
D'Artagnan and the Cardinal, in which the craft
and avarice of the Italian are matched by the ambition and dexterity of the man from Béarn. Possibly
the Mazarin of Courtilz de Sandras is unhistorical.
What does it matter, when the novel holds the attention to the last? He is in any case the Mazarin of
popular legend, the Cardinal about whom those
sheaves of Mazarinades were written, the Harpagon
who literally *smells* gold and in whom every human
sentiment is dead, yet who plays ducks and drakes
with the peace of Europe to secure imposing alliances
for his brood of nieces. The tale of his intrigues is
alone sufficient to make the success of the book, but
with D'Artagnan as Mazarin's secret agent, these
Mémoires unfold a picture of manners which is well-
nigh cosmopolitan in scope. There is only one possible
ending to a story of this sort—the death of the hero,

who passes away gloriously at the siege of Maestricht, in a fray into which "he was led by his courage, since upon that day he was not on duty." "Il n'était pas de jour." How like D'Artagnan, and what an epitaph!

This alliance between biography and the novel is all to the advantage of the latter. In the sentimental, historical *nouvelle* one cannot but notice the line of cleavage between the characters and their *milieu*. The historical cadre is always an accessory, like the formal scenery of classic tragedy. Courtilz de Sandras, on the other hand, so intermingles history and character-portrayal, that the former becomes as indispensable a part of the main action as the latter. Further, by blending the trivial with the serious, he helps to break down the barrier between comedy and tragedy, which the theatre of the time so jealously preserved. The effect of this procedure, in which Sandras unconsciously imitated Préschac, was to widen the sphere of the novel, which now embraced a multiplicity of pictures drawn from many categories of society, and thus expressed the emotions and sentiments which lie within that field of human experience situated midway between tragedy and comedy. Finally, the novelist's style gained enormously in vigour, flexibility and naturalness. What a contrast, for instance, between the manner of Courtilz de Sandras and of Scarron, who with all his brilliance yet produces eventually an effect of strain and unreality. Sandras, who has not a tithe of Scarron's wit, contrives nevertheless to captivate the interest by his unfailing good humour and simple narrative style. With him one overlooks the absence of technique, in the discovery that here at last is a novelist who can tell a story.

Though not published until 1713, Hamilton's *Mémoires du Comte de Grammont* were written in 1704. This book constitutes a portrait rather than a life-history. In Hamilton's own words, the following was his scheme. "In a plan which aims at giving an idea of him of whom I write, the things which distinguish him will appear in these fragments just as they present themselves to my imagination, without regard to their importance. After all, what does it matter where one begins a portrait, provided that the assemblage of parts forms a whole which is a perfect reproduction of the original?" His object was to portray a man whose character is a medley of qualities and defects, of vices and virtues. The form of this biographical novel is not, however, that of the *récit personnel*, since the author claims to write at Grammont's dictation. Yet, when the scribe is Antoine Hamilton, that is to say one of the undisputed masters of French prose, the narrative is liable to possess all the alertness of direct speech.

Hamilton, unlike Courtilz de Sandras, ignores chronology. At the opening of these *Mémoires* he deftly sketches in his historical background. We discover Grammont at the siege of Turin, as always the centre of attraction. Impossible to be serious in the company of this prince of good fellows. "Il cherchait et portait partout la joie." With his boon companion Matta, another cheery irresponsible, the

chevalier entertains with the lavishness peculiar to
the habitually indebted. This is the first of a series
of brilliant impressions in which Hamilton gradually
exposes the character of his hero. It might well be
called "the Portrait of a very young Gentleman."
Then we have Grammont the perfect lover, *à la*
D'Urfé, but more reminiscent of Hylas than of
Céladon, a regular wolf in sheep's clothing. Here
again one realises the artistic value of Matta, who
acts as an excellent foil to Grammont. Matta is
a delightful creation. He is the supreme *gaffeur*,
whose blundering efforts at playing the squire of
dames earn him little save black looks from his
lady and sententious advice from the perfidious
and wily Grammont, who uses him as a decoy to
occupy the attention of an unwelcome and pedan-
tic husband. Grammont, like D'Artagnan, serves
Mazarin, but after a different fashion, that is usually
to the disadvantage of the Italian. But the hero's
good luck for once deserts him. Louis is for the
moment in love with one of the Queen-Mother's
maids of honour, Mlle de la Motte-Houdancourt.
Grammont's impish mind conceives the mad idea
of setting up as a rival to the king; not, indeed,
that he had ever previously noticed the lady. As
Hamilton puts it: "Ce fut alors qu'il s'aperçut que
si l'amour rend les conditions égales ce n'est pas
entre rivaux"; and Grammont is invited to remove
his person from France at once.

But such vicissitudes are all in a day's work.
Imperturbable he reappears, gay, smiling and witty,

the darling of the English court. The picture of manners of London society under Charles II. is a fascinating one, yet it scarcely recompenses the reader for the somewhat secondary rôle to which the hero is now relegated. On rare occasions he again occupies all the stage, but more often he acts merely as a connecting-link between the various amorous episodes which compose this, the major part of the *Mémoires*. He eventually marries the beautiful Miss Hamilton, sister of the writer. Here the author might have regaled us with the real ending to the romance, which is much more in keeping with the character of Grammont than the conventional *dénouement* to which, for family reasons, he was obliged to resort. In reality the fickle hero left England hurriedly, omitting the customary religious ceremony. Hotly pursued by the lady's brother, he was overtaken on the Calais road. "Chevalier," cried Hamilton, "have you not forgotten something?" "I beg your pardon, Chevalier," was the smiling retort, "I fancy I have forgotten to marry your sister!" and amiably he retraced his steps to repair the oversight.

The relationship between Courtilz, Hamilton and Lesage is more easily sensed than expressed. A comparative study of the works of these three writers reveals no mutual influence either in choice of subject or of background. All, however, reflect the new tendencies which began to tinge French thought during the closing years of the reign of Louis XIV. In all three we perceive a slackening of the rigid moral code and conventions which in the seventeenth century attached man to society. The careers of D'Artagnan, Grammont and Gil Blas imply that wit will raise its possessor as high as birth or wealth. As the novel becomes less aristocratic, we shall see the novelist exploit this theme, gradually plunging his hero lower in the social scale, in order to add interest to the story of his upward flight to fame or fortune. A humanising process is introduced into fiction by the three authors I have named. Abstract moralisings on men in general give way to a consideration of the life and adventures of an individual. In these narratives, a growing materialism echoes the spirit of the *libertins*. The airy persiflage of Hamilton, and the mordant wit of Lesage, reveal a changing attitude towards the vices and foibles of humanity. Contrast with their easy tolerance the austerity of a Pascal, or the dignified intransigence of a Bossuet. Their outlook, though not at all admirable from the standpoint of strict morality, is, however, immensely human. The unpardonable sin for them consists in deliberately running counter to nature, and here they join hands with the *libertins*, and of course with Molière and Horace. Human experience and the observed facts of life form the material of the novelist's study. His interest is centred on the thousand ways in which one man differs from another, rather than on the common traits which permit of facile generalisations on humanity. Hence, though the novel maintains a certain coherence owing to the continued presence of one outstanding character, a multiplicity of adventures and of descriptive details lend variety and movement to the picture of manners. The dawning cosmopolitanism of the eighteenth century is foreshadowed in the sketches of English society furnished by Courtilz de Sandras and the Franco-Scottish Hamilton, while Lesage, though still pandering to the old interest in Spain, takes us to Central America and to Canada. The idealistic cult of woman, too, makes way for a more reasonable though more materialistic attitude, and the fetish of filial obedience strikes these moderns as somewhat Gothic in its stringency, though indeed their natural irreverence is discreetly veiled. On the other hand, the cult of royalty continues with unabated vigour, though one observes that the bourgeois Lesage is more sparing of his eulogies than his aristocratic colleagues. Altogether the novel gains in breadth and in interest, since it becomes more representative of life.

Chronologically the first of his novels, Lesage's *Diable boiteux* (1707) is, compared to his greater work, what the artist's sketch-book is to the finished canvas. Though, as he admits, the title and idea were borrowed from the *Diablo cojuelo* of the Spaniard Guevara, he has recast the original into a new work. The fanciful conception of a bottle imp, Asmodée, who lays bare before the eyes of his liberator, Don Cleophas, the intimacies of metropolitan life, partakes more of the fairy-tale than of the novel. In 1707, however, such *motifs* were very popular. Hamilton, Perrault and Mme D'Aulnoy produced excellent work in this vein, so that Lesage was but availing himself of a passing fashion in literature. The kernel of the story is the picture of contemporary *mœurs*, the fascinating "procession of originals," as the author called it, whose antics distract and edify the invisible watchers. Here comparison with La Bruyère imposes itself upon the reader's mind, for it is as if we were witnessing the famous *Caractères* galvanised into action. Yet all due reserve must be made for a difference in manner which arises from a fundamental difference in the personalities of the two authors. Both criticise society, but La Bruyère is in deadly earnest, whilst Lesage preserves the imperturbable good humour of the confirmed sceptic. He is the greater etcher of the two, and achieves the finer line: La Bruyère leaves the acid a trifle too long on the plate. But the style of the author of the *Caractères* announces that of Lesage, the same crisp, well-balanced phrase with a sting in its tail, the same simplicity of diction, yet with that impression of richness in vocabulary which is the result of a consummate knowledge of word values.

The comparison between Lesage and Molière has often been made, and for obvious reasons. They have in common a talent for observation, and a gift for extracting from a situation the element of universal and perennial truth. Naturally the novelist, owing to the peculiar facilities afforded by his genre, is enabled to present a more detailed picture of life than the dramatist. It is frequently said of Balzac that he is the first to portray "conditions" as opposed to *caractères*, that is, to present men in relation to their particular callings rather than in relation to life in general. This is only half true. Whilst Lesage, like Molière, gives us the miser, the hypocrite and the braggart, he also limns in unforgettable colours the poet, the doctor, the actress and the old soldier. Unlike Balzac, he confines himself to a general outline. We look in vain for the hundred traits that go to create a *milieu*. The truth is that Lesage the comic author and Lesage the novelist are constantly striving for supremacy. A description which seems to promise an interesting picture of eighteenth-century manners culminates as often as not in a brilliant *scène de comédie*. It is easy to detect here the influence of Lesage's literary ancestors Scarron and Molière. Realism in the nineteenth-century sense is almost entirely absent from his work: he is of the seventeenth century in this respect, that with him realism is a prelude to comedy or farce. It is for this reason that the well-known controversy as to the nationality of *Gil Blas* seems so futile. The consensus of opinion now points to the fact that *Gil Blas* owes little to Spain save its historical disguise. Critics have furnished "keys" which appear to prove that Triaquero is Voltaire, that Sangrado is modelled on a Doctor Hecquet, and that the *bureau d'esprit* of Mme de Chaves is intended for the *salon* of Mme de Lambert. Nothing is more probable, yet, if we accept the implication underlying such assertions, we shall be certainly led astray in our estimate of Lesage's novel. *Gil Blas* is not essentially a novel of manners in a national or local sense. It is not primarily, like the work of

Balzac or of Maupassant, a picture of French society, but rather a magnificent representation of universal society. And here it is that we discover the secret of the success of *Gil Blas*.

The notorious brigand Captain Rolando, in relating the unedifying story of his early struggles, tells how under the tuition of a rascally preceptor he became a *garçon universel*. How well the epithet applies to Gil Blas himself. "Seigneur de Santillane," cries the admiring Nunez, the poet, "vous avez l'outil universel, c'est à dire vous êtes propre à tout." And what indeed is the whole novel but a narrative of the hero's dexterity in adapting his pliant nature to a series of circumstances that change with kaleidoscopic rapidity. He is the universal trimmer whose characteristic is adaptability. Considered from this point of view, he will be seen to possess all the traits which make up the character of the trimmer, if such an agglomeration of unstable idiosyncrasies can be said to constitute a character in the moral sense of the term. He is extremely versatile. Doctor, apprentice, highwayman, valet, steward, secretary to an archbishop—is there a post which he cannot occupy with competence? Naturally obliging — I prefer the French word *serviable* — he is, like Don Raphael, another of his pleasant acquaintances, just as ready to do a good action as a bad one. And the impulse to oblige, though it frequently leads him into sorry scrapes, is never entirely quenched by the cold douche of experience. Too often the reader is repelled by the sordidness of the motives he alleges for his quixotic altruism, but always just in time Gil Blas reveals a sunny side to that very human, complex nature of his which disarms all but the most austere. He has the amour-propre of the young man who prides himself on being a very knowing fellow. The cardinal sin in his queer decalogue is that of being duped by someone sharper than himself. Yet along with this there goes a large tolerance which is wanting in the Puritan. When the fair-weather friend to whom he confides his disgrace with the archbishop assumes a cold, detached air and abruptly leaves him, the cynical ingratitude does not arouse in Gil Blas any deep emotions of disgust, or elicit from him scorching generalisations on men and adders. "I merely laughed at his ingratitude and looked at him with the contempt he deserved." And after all, who is Gil Blas to throw the first stone?

This *garçon universel* is a cynic. Life for him is a thronged market-place where men are hucksters engaged in the absorbing game of outdoing each other. Another Figaro, he has the perpetual air of one who comes into a crowded room crying: "Well, who is being 'done' to-day?" His attitude towards women is that of Anatole France, that is to say, the half-respectful, half-mocking manner of the eighteenth century. Most women are "fines mouches," amusing enough to pass an idle hour with, but dangerous as permanent attachments. It is the point of view of the man whose experience of the other sex is limited to the society of actresses and coquettes, for virtuous

women are as rare in Gil Blas' career as roses in
December. Still, he has the professional's admiration
for those other "*caméléons* qui changent de couleur
suivant l'humeur ou le génie des hommes qui les
approchent." His skirmishes with them have taught
him to be wary, but vanity lulls his watchfulness and
he is caught again. Some critic once pointed to the
failure of Gil Blas to profit from experience as one
of the chief inconsistencies in Lesage's creation. What
a strange illusion and what touching belief in the per-
fectibility of man! On the contrary, I regard this
"defect" as one of the most probable and therefore
most human characteristics of Gil Blas.

Another judgment often canvassed by detractors
of Lesage is the unlikelihood that so many vicissitudes
could fall within the range of one lifetime, a sage
observation were it applied to a serious young bourgeois of the twentieth century. Admittedly there is
much in the intercalated stories which stud this
novel that is improbable even from the seventeenth-
century point of view. But if we overlook these
concessions to a rapidly vanishing taste for the ultra-
romanesque, an element which must exist in every
good novel, there is little in Gil Blas' adventures
which we can condemn on the charge of improbability.
What offends us more to-day is the abuse of the
"recognition" device and the annoying contemporary
trick of making every new character relate his life-
story from birth onwards. However, it ill becomes
an English critic to cavil at this, since it was our
eighteenth-century novelists who introduced the dis-

tressing custom of anticipating life itself by pursuing their investigations into the dim regions of prenativity. Technically, then, and judged from present-day standards, Gil Blas is not perfect. Lesage, though he opens a new chapter in the evolution of the French novel, reveals traces of the seventeenth century, which is quite comprehensible when we reflect that he was born in 1668, and that he followed close on the heels of Scarron, Molière and Furetière. When he wrote *Gil Blas* the mania for Spanish literature and customs had not abated. He translated, or rather adapted, picaresque novels by Quevedo, Mateo Aleman and Obregon, and of course immediately drew upon himself accusations of plagiarism. Voltaire maliciously started the rumour that *Gil Blas* was a translation of a lost Spanish original, and raised a controversy the dust of which has but lately subsided. The verdict is that the originality of Lesage's creation remains unchallenged. " Je prends mon bien où je le trouve, " he might have said with Molière, and, like Molière's, his reputation rests upon three qualities—an unlimited power of observation, a respect for truth, and a *vis comica* unsurpassed by any other novelist in the whole field of European letters. And here we are reminded that Lesage is that rare genius, the comic author and the novelist in one, a dual gift as dangerous to handle as a two-edged sword. Yet how magnificently does he use it in *Gil Blas!* No one in modern times, save Anatole France, has been able to approach him. *Gil Blas* abounds in scenes which could be transported bodily behind the footlights. To cite two at random:

Gil Blas' interview with the Archbishop of Grenada, and Ambroise, disguised as an Inquisitor, examining the innkeeper Lamela regarding the Jew Samuel Simon. Here the dialogue moves with rapidity, crispness and naturalness. Molière himself could not better it.

Lesage is a realist, but in the widest sense of the term, for, while he has all the objectivity of the nineteenth-century school, he retains the seventeenth-century preference for the bold suggestive trait, as opposed to the minute brushwork of the moderns. Like them he is a picturesque realist, but to a lesser degree, since he lacks their colour and insistence on atmosphere. He is an etcher, not a painter. Occasionally, it is true, he will linger over the description of a banquet, for he loves good cheer, but usually he impatiently breaks with descriptive writing in order to pursue the narrative of adventures. Thus, "At this juncture I have an opportunity to give you a fine description of a tempest . . . but leaving aside all these 'fleurs de rhétorique,' I will tell you that the storm was violent." On the other hand, neither is he a psychological realist. He faithfully observes the actions and retails the sayings and reflections of his characters. In his inimitable fashion he comments and moralises on their adventures, but makes little attempt to examine their origins. In other words, he is a moralist, not a psychologist. "Personne n'est plus sûr moraliste que Lesage," says Faguet; "personne n'est moins psychologue." He has the moralist's love for the sententious generalisation. "Un flatteur peut

tout risquer avec les grands "; "Il avait l'esprit
décisif comme l'ont la plupart des petits hommes ";
"Un fripon peut fort bien devenir un honnête
homme "; "Une femme excuse jusqu'aux mauvaises
actions que sa beauté fait commettre ": epigrammatic
phrases which remind us that we have just left the
century which produced a La Rochefoucauld and a
La Bruyère. Lesage's realism is that of the observer
whose eyes are ruthlessly riveted on the foibles and
eccentricities of mankind. His picture of society
affects the critic in strangely different ways. One's
estimate of *Gil Blas* varies according to one's own
experience of the world. The idealist may dismiss
the novel impatiently as a calumny on human nature,
but on reflection he cannot deny that Lesage's picture
of the average man is a true one. The author, like
Molière, utters no great philosophical truths. He has
no profound lesson to offer save that which teaches
us not to make fools of ourselves, and that, as some
critic of Molière once pertinently remarked, is no
morality at all. The object of Lesage is that of the
comic author, to amuse and instruct. His motto is
"ridendo castigo." Possibly *Gil Blas* is losing its
appeal. We live in an age which has a passion for
"improving" literature. We tend to become impatient
of a book which does not convey the message of some
new gospel or the promise of some dazzling Utopia.
But some day we shall recover our lost sense of
perspective and at the same time our sense of humour.
Then *Gil Blas* will come back to its own.

CHAPTER V

THE half-century from 1680 till 1730 is a fascinating period from the point of view of the literary historian. French tragedy, which had reached its apogee with Racine, slowly sinks into oblivion. Poetry, her wings neatly clipped by Boileau, must await the dawn of Romanticism before resuming her upward flight. The shadow of Molière's genius lies athwart the new century and, with the sole exception of Marivaux, there is no one to carry on the evolution of comedy. Is it by mere coincidence or by the operation of some hidden law of reciprocity that the novel, benefiting from the stagnation of the other literary genres, chooses just this period to enter on a further stage of its development? We have already seen that the novelist, conscious of the object of his art, which is to produce the reflection and the illusion of life, did not hesitate to borrow freely from tragedy, comedy and history such artistic methods of procedure as could be conveniently transferred to his own genre. That he did so with advantage we know from the works of Scarron, Lafayette, Lesage and Hamilton, whose writings reveal a rising degree of probability in the imitation of human sentiments and actions. Further, the novelist's field of observation has widened. We shall discuss in a later chapter the fascinating voyage of discovery which led the French novelist outside his own country, both in reality and in imagination, in order to satisfy the curiosity of a nation eager for details on the manners and customs of the foreigner.

Meanwhile let us consider the contribution made to the history of the evolution of the French by l'abbé Prévost. His life, like that of his heroes, offers strange and fascinating contradictions. Born with clerical and scholarly inclinations, Prévost was for twenty years the plaything of a restless and romantic temperament. In turn Benedictine monk, soldier, wanderer and monk again, this Ishmael of literature eventually found his good angel in the person of the prince de Conti, who in 1743 engaged him as chaplain. Prévost lived by his pen, a fact which must be considered in estimating his work, since it explains several of his defects. The temptation to be diffuse is very great when one is paid by the page.

Prévost continues the school of Mme de Lafayette, but except for his immortal *Manon Lescaut*, he wrote novels and not *nouvelles*. He invariably affected the form of the *récit personnel*, which suited his simple conversational style, and produces the illusion, if it is one, that we are listening to a confession, for so striking is the resemblance between the Prévost of biography and his principal characters, that it is difficult to forget that we are dealing with an age when subjective writing was not yet in fashion. Though probably better educated than Lesage, l'abbé

Prévost carries his erudition lightly. He does not, like the author of *Gil Blas*, parade his classical lore, an annoying trick of so many French men of letters. His historical knowledge was obviously vast, however, and he situates four of his novels in the period of the English Civil Wars, with which he was thoroughly familiar.

Prévost's literary ancestors are to be sought chiefly in the novelists of the late seventeenth century, and in Racine. He preferred the old heroic novels to the sentimental historical productions which succeeded them, excepting always *La Princesse de Clèves*. "En voulant peindre les hommes au naturel, on y fait des portraits trop charmants de leurs défauts," he says, commenting on the modern school, which he contrasts most unfavourably with the heroic novelists, who at least depicted noble sentiments and were irreproachable from the moral point of view. There can be no question as to Prévost's sincerity here, for he is one of the few early eighteenth-century novelists who realised the moral responsibility which attaches to the trade of author. Prévost's outlook on life is fundamentally Calvinist or Jansenist, which is much the same thing, and here we must recollect the great influence exercised on his work by the tragedies of Racine, whom he passionately admired. It is significant, too, that, in his *Histoire d'une Grecque moderne* (1740), Prévost's hero, when confronted with the problem of educating his mistress Théophé according to the best tenets of French morality, gives her the *Essais de Nicole* and *La Logique du Port Royal*.

But Prévost is only half a Jansenist. Whilst he believes, like Port Royal, that man's greatest enemy
is passion, he is too imbued with the philosophic
ideas of his age to hold any great belief in the saving
power of grace. For him the only antidote to the
overwhelming force of a great passion is reason, and
so we find in this author the curious reconciliation
of two antagonistic philosophies, the attempt of an
eighteenth-century writer to adapt the newly acquired
ideas of the English Deists to the austere religious
principles imbibed by him in early youth.

Now the classic restraint of Racine had already
begun to lose its appeal for the public of the Regency.
The general relaxation of morals was accompanied
inevitably by a lowering of æsthetic standards. A
public which lives to gratify the senses desires a
literature which will make its appeal through the
same channels. Already the violent and terrible
tragedies of Crébillon *père* had captured popular
fancy, and French tragedy swiftly descended to the
level of melodrama. Prévost's ardent temperament,
avid of sensations and prone to view the blacker
side of life, was all the more exposed to such influence
by reason of his residence in England, whither he
escaped from the cloister in 1728. In the second part
of the *Mémoires d'un Homme de Qualité* (1731), the
author expresses his unqualified admiration for
English tragedy, for "that tragic form which stirs
the depths of the heart and which infallibly excites
the passions in the most sluggish soul, by the force
of expression and the art of conducting the action

and handling situations. I have read nothing in Greek or in French," he continues, "which excels the English theatre." Prévost's favourite plays were *Hamlet*, Dryden's *Don Sebastian* and Otway's *Venice Preserved*. That being so, the most horrible of Crébillon's plays must have seemed very mild indeed to Prévost's sombre imagination. This very early sojourn in England, at the very outset of his literary career, is of great importance. If we ignore it, it is impossible to understand the un-French character of his novels, although, as I have tried to show, the influence of English tragedy but served to strengthen and to consolidate tendencies which were inherent in Prévost's nature, and which moreover formed part of the spirit of the France of the seventeen-twenties. Later we shall see that Prévost again visited England, and it is at that stage that we must consider the influence exerted upon his work by the English novel, particularly since it was the abbé Prévost who translated and popularised Richardson in France.

The essential link between the novels of Prévost and tragedy is the preponderating rôle assigned to fate. We may best grasp this by contrasting Lesage's *Gil Blas* with Cleveland, the sombre hero of the abbé's *Le Philosophe anglais ou Histoire de M. Cleveland* (1731–9). As in tragedy, Prévost's central character is predestined to unhappiness. From the first page to the last he is "the most unfortunate of men." Where Gil Blas deftly adapts himself to the changing circumstances of life, Cleveland, convinced of the futility of resistance, opposes, but in a very half-hearted way, what he conceives to be the buffetings of fate. The final issue is never in doubt. We know from the outset, and we are constantly reminded of the fact, that Cleveland can never find true happiness. It is true that Prévost, as an afterthought and as a sop to clerical prejudice, leaves his free-thinking hero safe in the arms of the Church, but in doing so he convinces neither himself nor his reader.

In his *Histoire d'une Grecque moderne* he is more logical. We know from the opening chapter that the hero is fated never to win the love of the woman whom he has rescued and educated, and the ending which leaves him unloved and hopeless is in the spirit of true tragedy. In his fatalism Prévost follows the tradition of Greek tragedy rather than of French neo-classicism, but in his conception of the passion of love he is Racinian. In his novels love is depicted as a swiftly rising and devouring passion. It is the insidious enemy of man, ever on the watch to surprise and overpower reason and virtue. It destroys character as a powerful acid corrodes metal, and having once disposed of reason, it brings in its train parricide, suicide, murder and rape. In *Cleveland* there is a striking example of the terrible effects of love in the character of Gelin, an honourable, intelligent and impetuous Frenchman who conceives a violent passion for the wife of Cleveland. Originally a close friend of the hero, Gelin stirs up jealousy in the mind of Cleveland's wife, Fanny. He persuades her to elope with him, murders Cleveland's brother, and finally attempts the life of his former friend.

In the *Mémoires de M. de Montcal* (1741), the heroine, Mlle Fidert, kills her own father to avenge her lover, and stabs Montcal in a fit of jealousy. Indeed, in all Prévost's novels there is scarcely an instance of happy love. Happiness, if it finally comes, is procured always at the cost of suffering, remorse and bloodshed. From this point of view, of course, Prévost is a writer of *romans à thèse*. His thesis is that love and happiness are incompatible. Man's only salvation lies in the pursuit of reason. That is why all his heroes are *philosophes*. In the *Mémoires d'un honnête Homme* (1745), the hero falls in love with the wife of his dearest friend, who is a confirmed invalid. This is how he combats his passion:

It was not the fear of lacking control over myself and of making myself contemptible in the eyes of Mme de B. and of her husband which forced me to recall all the strength of my reason, but realising that the disorder of my heart was affecting my health, lacking appetite and having lost all desire to sleep and all taste for the most agreeable amusements, I was ashamed of myself for a weakness whose effects were so dangerous. I reduced the whole question to this reasoning. There is no inclination, however sweet, no illusion, however flattering, which can make me violate the rights of hospitality and marriage. It is a sacred duty which suffers no exception in my principles. All that remains for me is the secret pleasure of sentiment, but here I no longer experience anything but cruel torture. The natural progress of such a violent alteration can only be now the loss of my health and reason. I must renounce it.

In their relations to society, then, Prévost's heroes try to practise the new ideas which the eighteenth-century philosophers are beginning to disseminate. The hero of the *Mémoires d'un Homme de Qualité*, for instance, loses no opportunity of moralising for the benefit of his young pupil, the marquis. He bids him move among all classes of the people. The poor man, "en qualité d'homme," has the same rights as the aristocrat to the sweets of rest and abundance. It is chance alone which decides that one should be born to happiness and another to misery. He moralises on the social vices of gambling, prostitution and duelling, and reflects pessimistically on the uselessness of experience in a society where man is at the mercy of passion. The philosopher Cleveland is convinced of the innate corruption of man, and the reader who follows his experiences through five volumes finds his pessimism extremely natural. One must not, however, forget that Cleveland is an Englishman, and to the eighteenth-century French novelist all Englishmen, like Cleveland, are introspective, sombre, and prone to suicide. All have that "horreur invincible de la vie" which Prévost like other French writers regards as climatic.

Prévost is a humanitarian, and consequently a cosmopolitan. The second part of his *Mémoires d'un Homme de Qualité* is a long eulogy of English manners, customs and ideas. At a time when England, outside London, was practically unknown to the French, he urges his fellow-countrymen to cross the Channel, rid themselves of their prejudices, and discover an England different from the commercial, hard and perfidious Albion of legend. Save for the populace, which is rude and ferocious, the English, unlike the Spaniards, "gagnent à être connus." Prévost praises the English love of the commonweal, their horror

for slavery, and their predilection for the solid sciences.
It is usual to say of Prévost that he had no eye for
"la vérité pittoresque." It is true that in general he
is not concerned with externals in his descriptions
of manners, but we must make a notable exception
in the case of the second volume of these *Mémoires*.
Here the picture of *mœurs* is detailed, vivid and
penetrating. It is easy to see that during his sojourn
the author visited Oxford, Bristol, Bath, Plymouth,
Tunbridge Wells, since his descriptions of these places
are gleaned, not from his reading, but from direct
observation. His comments on Spanish manners, however, are not so convincing, and are gleaned, I fear,
from literature.

There is an imaginative episode in *Cleveland* which
is very typical of Prévost and the new spirit of the
eighteenth century. On a remote island near St.
Helena, the hero discovers an ideal community composed of Huguenot refugees. In this Utopian state
all property is common, though what the chevalier
d'Arcq called "the harmonious inequality of the
classes" is preserved. No one is allowed to carry arms,
and all marriage is by lot, a necessity on an island
where the scarcity of husbands is distressingly acute.
Adultery is punishable by death. It is significant
that Prévost attributes the breaking up of this ideal
state to the perfidy and fanaticism of the Protestant
Church, as personified by a pastor who, on finding
that several of his flock have contracted secret
marriages, proceeds to punish the culprits for daring
to obey the laws of natural selection.

In America, Cleveland finds in the Ibaquas the ideal savages of eighteenth-century fiction, and on becoming their chief, educates them according to the principles of Deism. His community is organised on military lines, and is governed by a general council of the elders into which women are admitted, for, as the author infers, when women have passed the age of love they are no longer the blind victims of passion and may be consulted with profit.

In Prévost's novels there is always a woman in love who makes overtures to the hero. Long before the Romantics, this author expressed the belief that "Une lutte éternelle . . . se livre . . . entre la bonté de l'Homme et la ruse de la Femme." Lady R., the victim of a cruel husband, throws herself on the generosity of the Homme de Qualité: Cleveland is pursued by a Mme Lallin. Montcal is passionately loved and temporarily seduced from the path of virtue by Mlle Fidert. The Honnête Homme receives a letter from his father's second wife saying that she has guessed the reason for her stepson's hurried departure, and assuring him that she will remain true. This curious obsession of Prévost's had its origin possibly in the author's own experience. His great enemy, Lenglet du Fresnoy, published a story which was believed by many, though denied by Prévost. It was to the effect that the abbé was seduced in Holland by an unknown lady, who persuaded him to elope with her to England. I think, however, that quite apart from this legend we can find ample reasons for Prévost's attitude in his early religious training,

and in his acquired Jansenist outlook. To the novelist
and artist also the theme is an attractive one, and
well calculated to arouse the reader's interest, and
it is obvious why Prévost makes so much capital out
of these moral conflicts in the minds of his heroes,
who need all the strength of their philosophy to
struggle against feminine onslaughts.

His men, however, are not always passive. Love
comes to them in a flash. It is a *coup de foudre* which
benumbs the reason and destroys all principles of
conduct. Henceforth nothing counts in life save what
directly affects the object of their passion. And here
it seems to me we have the greatness of Prévost. Here
he is absolutely true to life. The most famous of his
heroes, the Des Grieux of the immortal *Manon Lescaut*,
typifies for all time this conception of the devastating
effects of a great passion. The story is simple. A young
man, gently bred and of studious habits, is waiting
for the Arras stage-coach. It comes, bringing into his
life inconceivable misery and exquisite happiness. A
beautiful girl alights, and Des Grieux, who has never
thought of women, can now conceive no life possible
without Manon. They elope, and for a time live
happily. But Manon, though she loves her chevalier,
must have luxury. She secretly becomes the mistress
of a rich financier. To her this physical lapse is of
very little account, since her heart is still with Des
Grieux, but to him the betrayal is apostasy. The
chevalier is taken home by his father and resumes
his studies. Soon he is on the way to fame, for he has
the golden gift of oratory. But one day Manon comes

to the church of St. Sulpice, and Des Grieux gives up
parents, friends and career to follow her again. After
that the descent is swift. The lover commits murder
to release Manon from prison, but she is captured
and sentenced to deportation as a prostitute. Shattered morally and physically, her faithful chevalier
follows her to America, only to see her die. He buries
her in the desert and returns to France.

Such, in a few words, is the brief outline of a story
which has inspired poets, artists and musicians. It
is Prévost's masterpiece, and one of the three classics
of the French novel of the eighteenth century. Austere
moralists have taken exception to the ending, where
Manon, by her death, is purified and etherealised: "ce
beau mensonge du poète," as one French critic has
so well described it. How Prévost would have grieved
at the suggestion that his book was dangerous; poor
Prévost, whose constant purpose was to warn youth
against the dangers of unbridled passion. Yet such
is the strange appeal of his simple beautiful prose,
such is the *naïveté* of his sentiments, so idealised is
the illicit love of Manon and Des Grieux, that their
unhappy story has captured popular sympathy and
won for them a place in literature higher than that
accorded to the chaste Paul and Virginia. Prévost is
a sentimentalist and a moralist, but in *Manon Lescaut*
he has struck that note of restraint and sympathy
which raises him head and shoulders above Richardson
and Rousseau. If one wishes to realise the contrast
between true sentiment and mawkish *sensiblerie*, let
him read *Manon* and *Pamela*. Not that Prévost can-

not be mawkish too. In the *Mémoires d'un honnête
Homme*, and in his *Monde moral* (1760), there are pages
of insufferable priggishness and crocodile sentiment,
but it is only fair to say that he wrote these after
having begun his monumental labour of translating
Richardson. But in his earlier novels he can be sentimental without insincerity, though his sentiment
usually assumes a morbid tinge. At sixty, l'Homme
de Qualité discovers to his shame that his heart is
still vulnerable, and only the memory of his dead wife
preserves him from yielding to the advances of the
enterprising Lady R. It is their sentimentality and
quixotic generosity which lead Prévost's heroes into
equivocal situations and make them the dupes of
adventurous women, who play upon their misguided
sense of honour. In young Cleveland the author has
drawn a beautiful portrait of a boy in love. Educated
by his mother to believe that philosophy is the only
shield against the passions, and starved of maternal
affection, he is indeed, as he says, "one of those unhappy children on whom their parents have never
smiled." Prévost's description of the dawning of love
in Cleveland is one of his finest achievements, and
places him with Marivaux amongst the earliest
psychological novelists.

Prévost's sensibility reveals itself most frequently
in his fondness for death-bed scenes, but his vivid
imagination is not content with mere pathos. He
revels in harrowing and morbid descriptions. Dreams,
premonitions, burials at dead of night in subterranean
passages, rooms tapestried with black, heroines shut

up by ferocious husbands in company with a corpse—
all the stock in trade of the Romantic dramatists is
to be found in Prévost's novels. Many years before
Baculard d'Arnaud he introduced the *genre sombre*
into French literature. "It seems as if my sadness
communicates itself to all nature," says Cleveland,
"and as if all that surrounds me grieves and sorrows
on my behalf." And again, describing the secret
nocturnal marriages on the isle of refugees, he expresses
the same feeling of man's communion with nature,
a feeling which is essentially Romantic. "La lune
semblait s'être ornée de toute sa lumière pour éclairer
un spectacle digne de l'attention du Ciel et de la
Terre et par un effet sans doute de l'extrême satisfaction de mon cœur qui se répandait en quelque
sorte sur toute la nature l'air ne m'avait jamais paru
si doux ni la verdure si riante que pendant le reste
de cette charmante nuit." True, such passages are
rare in Prévost, yet they acquire significance when
we realise that they were written in 1731, and indicate
the dawnings of a new feeling for external nature,
thirty years before the appearance of Rousseau's
Nouvelle Héloïse. It is interesting to speculate on the
sources of this new sentiment in the novel, and, as
always in such cases, the critic is tempted to look
to foreign influences for an explanation. However, in
this particular instance, I feel that we must discount
any theory of Anglo-French interaction and examine
the works of Prévost himself. This desire for communion with nature is simply an extension of a craving
for sympathy which characterises nearly all his

heroes. Cleveland in the caves of Rumney Hole is seized with an irresistible longing for human friendship. Deprived of this solace, he spends his time carving inscriptions on the walls of his retreat. "Ma douleur semble se décharger en s'exprimant," he explains. He broods over his sorrows, committing them to paper, so as to preserve their memory and inspire a sympathetic sadness in the susceptible hearts of his readers. Cleveland is a precocious René, morbidly introspective and profoundly convinced of the "intolerable emptiness" of existence. But here we must make reserves. The source of Cleveland's misery is tangible. His pessimism is inspired by the illusion that his wife has betrayed him. His malady is curable since its cause can be discerned, whilst in the case of René only death can cure the ill which has its roots in the fact that he exists.

The pre-Romanticism of Prévost's novels, then, must be regarded as an extension of his sensibility, the effusion of a heart which, thanks to the illusion of a vivid imagination, finds not only in man, but in nature, a sympathetic response to its outpourings.

There is in the work of Prévost another element which we must not confuse with the above. Cleveland's wife, Fanny, who is convinced by the perfidious Gelin of her husband's infidelity, longs for some "asyle écarté, quelque antre sauvage ou quelque tombeau dont l'entrée ne soit pas interdite à la douleur et à la vertu. . . . Un antre! le plus profond, le plus obscur, le plus conforme à l'état de ma fortune et aux tristes sentiments de mon âme." Do not let ourselves be deceived by rhetoric. This is of course a new language, for Prévost is the predecessor of Diderot. But *le romanesque*, even when expressed in the violent, picturesque idiom of the eighteenth century, is not Romanticism. Already, in the *Princesse de Clèves*, a bruised heart longed for solitude and found it very simply in the cloister. Fanny does not feel more deeply than Mme de Clèves: she merely arrives at a period in the evolution of the novel when it is no longer "bad form" or bad literary taste to retail the innermost yearnings of the soul. This style of Prévost's is pre-Romantic: his ideas are still *romanesque*, and that, as we have seen, is by no means new in the novel, since we can trace it back to the Middle Ages.

Prévost was one of the first novelists to realise the pathetic possibilities of the convent, though he did not exploit them to the fullest extent. Those precocious *Lettres d'une Religieuse portugaise* ought to have aroused him more thoroughly to the potentialities of the cloister as a source of tragedy. On the other hand, it is very probable that, having spent a considerable part of his life in one, he was handicapped by his lack of ignorance. One cannot for instance conceive of an intelligence-officer writing a really thrilling spy story. To some extent the novelist must always retain the objective, ignorant and popular standpoint of the reader. It is difficult to weave romance into those experiences which we wish to forget, and that I think explains Prévost's silence.

CHAPTER VI

In 1753 Diderot, in one of those crises of anglomania which were apt to befog his critical faculties, held up Fielding's *Amelia* as an admirable example of *le roman domestique*, a species of novel, said he, which was quite unknown in France. He was good enough, however, to absolve his compatriots from any suspicion of being lacking in genius: the fault, he asserted, lay not in that, but rather in the fact that the French had no domestic life to describe. So far he was guilty merely of an unsuccessful paradox, but when we find him maintaining that the fashionable and lubricous novels of Crébillon *fils* reflect the average domestic life of the French nation, we can but marvel at the excesses of which a luminous mind is capable when it is temporarily fascinated by the literature of a foreign country. Had Diderot not been so obsessed by the Englishmen Richardson and Fielding, he must surely have done justice to Pierre de Marivaux, who, in his *Vie de Marianne* (1731–41) and in his *Paysan parvenu* (1735–6), inaugurated in France the domestic novel which the authors of *Pamela* and *Amelia* later exploited with such conspicuous success. Some modern critics indeed maintain that *Marianne* in-

spired Richardson's *Pamela*, and point to the similarity of the themes of *Le Paysan parvenu* and
Joseph Andrews as a proof that Fielding, too, was
indebted to the genial Frenchman. Fräulein Schröers,
a German critic, has made a minute page by page
comparison of *Marianne* and *Pamela* to prove her
thesis. All that results, however, from this painstaking effort is the discovery that, if two writers
start with the hypothesis that a lonely girl is subjected
to temptation, they will discover that many of her
experiences will be surprisingly like those of another
girl in the same circumstances. In the words of
Boileau: "La raison pour marcher n'a souvent qu'une
voie." An examination of Richardson's unpublished
correspondence reveals a complete indifference to
French literature. Fielding, on the other hand, had
read Marivaux and most of the French contemporary
novelists, but there is little indication that he was
influenced by *Le Paysan parvenu*. The one outstanding quality of Marivaux's style is his originality, and
even if a writer of Fielding's individuality had been
prone to borrow, he would certainly have avoided an
author whose genius was so unique as to enrich the
French language with the term *marivaudage*.

A backward glance at the French novelists who
preceded Marivaux reveals few who can be really
called novelists of manners. Scarron, Furetière, and
to a lesser extent Lesage, provide glimpses into the
family life of certain sections of French society. But,
as we have seen, few of their pictures are far re-
moved from caricature. They choose characters who

ill-represent the particular condition or profession to which they are said to belong. Truth is sacrificed to satire, and what in the comic author is a virtue becomes a defect in the novelist. It was Marivaux who first showed that the novelist might reflect the *mœurs* of contemporary society without necessarily being as grotesque as Scarron or as suggestive as Crébillon the younger. His *Marianne* is the story of the adventures of a nameless girl who, after many vicissitudes, eventually takes that place in society to which, we find, she was entitled by birth. *Le Paysan parvenu*, as the title suggests, is the account of the rise to fortune of a young peasant, who owes his success partly to his external attractions and in a large measure to his native wit and unscrupulousness.

At a time when French literature was extremely aristocratic, it needed some courage to base two entire novels on the hypothesis that rank and wealth are not essential to social advancement. It is true that Marivaux somewhat shirks the issue by giving as sub-title to *Marianne*, "les mémoires de la duchesse de x x." His second novel, however, makes no concession to prejudice, and justifies his gibe at the snobbery of the average novel reader who wants only "l'histoire du cœur dans les grandes conditions." A famous passage in *Marianne*, and one which caused considerable embarrassment to Marivaux's sponsor when the former was received into the Académie française, was that containing the excellent description of Marianne's experiences as lodger in the house of Mme Dutour the seamstress. Balzac has done

nothing better than this realistic study of a little
bourgeois *milieu*. The portrait of Mme Dutour, the
inquisitive, vain, kindly gossip, is unforgettable. No
one can read it and doubt that Mme Dutour existed
as she exists to-day in the rue Antoine or in the
rue Sainte-Anne. The memorable quarrel with the
"cabby" is one of the most humorous and most
life-like studies in the whole of French literature.
How odd that it should be Marivaux, the author
of the exquisite comedies *Les fausses Confidences*
and *Le Jeu de l'Amour et du Hasard*, who should give
us the first foretaste of nineteenth-century realism
in the French novel! But it would be easy to ex-
aggerate the importance of this aspect of his work
as a novelist. His perfect reproduction of atmosphere, which is to be accounted for partly by his
meticulous attention to external details like *milieu*,
conversation and gesture, depends chiefly on his
insight into the minds of his subjects. In a word,
Marivaux is *par excellence* a psychologist and one of
the greatest in the history of the French novel.

To understand his peculiar method of approach, let
us examine his analysis of the character of Marianne.
The young girl is a never-ending source of interest
to Marivaux, as she is to Marcel Prévost and Marcel
Proust. It is natural that this should be so. Marriage
exercises on the feminine mind a simplifying influence.
At first this sounds paradoxical, but not when we
stop to contemplate that beautiful chaos of contradictory emotions and caprices which constitute the
virginal mind, and which are collected and canalised

by marriage into two definite currents, maternity
and wifehood. It may be objected that the married
woman has formed the subject of many great psychological novels, notably Flaubert's *Madame Bovary*.
Yet, in the psychological sense, the Madame Bovarys
of the world are really unmarried, since matrimony
has failed in their case to perform the simplifying
operation to which I allude. In other words, we have
in women like Madame Bovary the tangle of whims,
desires and suppressions which make up the iridescent
fabric of a girlish mind like Marianne's.

The interest of *La Vie de Marianne* lies in the
spectacle of a young, intelligent and pretty girl, of
unknown origin, at grips with the prejudices of a
society which looks askance at young and charming
girls without dowries or credentials. Marianne is
shrewd and ambitious and clever. She is a born
coquette who is determined to get married, a formid-
able if not usually a particularly pleasant combination
of characteristics. But here Marivaux is an artist.
At the outset we see only a rather desperate little
girl anxious to secure a place in society; but when
she falls in love with Valville she captures our sympathy. Now her energies, which had hitherto been
governed by material motives, are concentrated on
one object—to please Valville and keep his love. Her
amour-propre, always delicate, now becomes intensely
susceptible because of the gulf between her social
position and that of her lover.

There is a rock-like quality about Marianne's
character which we must admire. She is of course

momentarily tempted by the hypocritical Climal, Valville's uncle, but the ultimate effect of his advances is to make her furious with the elderly Don Juan, since he compromises her in the eyes of his nephew. She is angry with Valville for his jealousy, which, to a woman so much in love, appears naturally absurd. Marivaux's picture of her here is fascinating. Her first fury gone, she pities herself and weeps for her dead parents, whom she cannot possibly remember. Then, for she is always ruthless in her self-analysis, she reflects: "Peut-être n'était-ce pas là ce que je voulais dire et ne parlais-je de mes parents que pour rendre le sujet de mon affliction plus honnête."

Marianne is the embodiment of youth, irrepressible yet easily despairing, as when she creeps into a church to cry for her lost Valville. Her meeting with the prioress and with Valville's mother occurs here, and gives Marivaux an excellent opportunity to contrast two different types of women, and to reveal Marianne's reactions to her new *milieu*, the convent. Valville's mother, Mme de Miran, is one of the sweetest women in French fiction. She represents what was, after all, the average aristocratic society of the eighteenth century, and it is good to dwell upon her gracious personality before we approach the so-called *romanciers corrupteurs*, Crébillon *fils*, La Morlière and others, whose women, though more obtrusive and more disturbing, constituted really a small section of polite society. Marianne's latent generosity of mind rushes up to respond to the winning kindness of Mme de Miran, and it is not wholly insincerity which prompts her to do all she can to dissuade Valville from marrying her and thus irritating his family. The fact is that her amour-propre is flattered at the rôle she is playing. She complacently regards her own *belle âme*, and when she hears herself saying " Je serai religieuse," she is, like all the onlookers, swept forward on the crest of an emotional wave, and what can the sentimental Mme de Miran do but cry out to her son: "Aime-la mon enfant!"?

Marivaux gives a delightful account of Marianne's fears, joys and doubts at this stage. She is calculating, but not objectionable, because she is fighting for love. Introduced into society, she is absolutely at her ease, because her amour-propre tells her that she has taste and tact. The instinct which prompts Marianne in her new surroundings is one of the strongest and most feminine traits laid bare by Marivaux. It is to a more intense degree the instinct which temporarily makes even a *cocotte* behave like a lady, a sort of social mimetism common to all intelligent women. In Marianne, however, it is exaggerated by love and by a natural ability to please. Marianne in society is a good psychological study, but it reveals Marivaux also as a painter of *mœurs* who has the power to depict groups and to convey to the reader the illusion of movement. He describes a society which frequented *salons* such as that of Mme de Lambert, who was one of the author's intimates. The keynote of the conversation of these people is politeness in the most literal acceptation of the term. The aristocracy here described is one not merely of birth but of wit. Marianne notices this fact. "C'étaient des hommes entre qui seulement les meilleures raisons l'emportaient sur les plus faibles; rien que cela."

With Marivaux the novel approaches for the first time Brunetière's definition of it as an *image sociale*. But *Marianne* and *Le Paysan parvenu* are by no means complete documents on the society of their time. They cannot be compared in this respect with the productions of Balzac, and we have seen why this is so. Yet Marivaux must be given credit for having carried the novel a step forward in its evolution. That he was gravely handicapped by contemporary criticism we have observed. His public, imbued with the literary traditions of the seventeenth century, had a fine classic scorn for these elements which we look for in the novel of to-day, details concerning the appearance, the daily habits and the *milieu* of the characters. Of course, in his efforts to reflect contemporary life, Marivaux is by no means a pioneer, but he is the first great novelist to essay a picture and not a caricature of the society of his day. His *Paysan parvenu*, for instance, contains the first truthful description of the *petite bourgeoisie* that we possess in the French novel. His etching of the sisters Habert, the two little well-fed old maids with their mock asceticism and devotion, while undershot with a certain sly humour, is true to life. In this connection the author is outspoken in his criticism of the *directeur de conscience*, and his easy, good-humoured smile vanishes while he arraigns these unworthy servants of the Church. Readers of *Marianne* will recollect also his indictment of the materialism and selfishness of the secular clergy. His picture of the world of finance is well executed. He rises above the mere satire of a Lesage, possibly because he had more real reason to know and to despise the financier than the author of *Gil Blas*. As is well known, Marivaux lost his whole fortune in the Mississippi speculation organised by that amazing adventurer John Law. Nevertheless his judgment remains perfectly balanced, and in *Le Paysan parvenu* we find the most dispassionate account of the social influence of the financier which it is possible to find in the novel of the eighteenth century. To simplify matters, he presents two types of financier, Bono and Fécour, who embody the chief characteristics of their class in 1735. It is obvious that the Turcaret generation has died out. Instead, we have Fécour the cold, ruthless and efficient administrator, the precursor of the *homme fort* of 1850. Retailed by Marivaux, an interview between this man and Jacob, the "paysan parvenu," becomes something more than an interesting episode: it is the clash of two classes. Rarely has the contrast between brutal materialism and sentimental generosity been so well brought out, as in the scene where Jacob refuses the offer of a place in favour of the husband of a lady whose distress has touched his impressionable heart. Marivaux is a sentimentalist and he foreshadows the humanitarian novel which reached its apogee about the seventies of the eighteenth century. In Jacob and in Bono, the other financier, he has embodied something of the new spirit which was to find its fullest expression in the writings of Rousseau and his followers. Yet Bono has something of the author's own diffidence. He is afraid of appearing ridiculous because of his humanity. Gruff, kindly and tactless, he owes his fortune to chance and to honesty rather than to the shady, clever methods of the average *fermier-général*.

Marivaux evidently intended Jacob as a sort of complement to Marianne. Both owe their social advancement to their natural gifts. Both represent the struggle between ambition and the passive resistance offered by society in such cases. But here the resemblance ceases, because the Jacobs of life will never succeed in conquering the hostility and prejudice which they excite in their own sex. The average male will always find something repulsive in the spectacle of a man who succeeds through feminine influence. Brunetière well expresses this popular feeling when he coins the epithet "un beau coq de village" for Marivaux's hero. Yet Jacob is largely a passive agent. By simply remaining natural, he is swept on by circumstances to success. The women do the rest. Marivaux tries sometimes to enlist our sympathy for his hero by emphasising his physical courage and his generosity, but the stigma refuses to disappear. And yet how true to life it all is! From chambermaid to *grande dame* all the women love Jacob, and they do not love him just for his physique. That is a false judgment repeated by every critic and one which, if not insulting to women, at least reveals a lack of understanding of the feminine

mind. Marivaux knows better. Jacob succeeds with
the other sex because it recognises in him a complete
absence of the usual male prejudice against taking
gifts from women. From Geneviève's few wretched
louis to Mme de Vambures' gift of a tax-farm, Jacob
accepts all, and he accepts with the nonchalance
of a sultan. Naturally the women love him for it.
Marivaux's analysis of this peasant's mind is exquisite.
As always he preserves apparent impartiality, and
almost forces us to admit qualities in his model
which in any other would arouse admiration. There
is no doubt, however, as to the final summing-up
which is contained in one lapidary phrase. I refer
to the passage in which he describes Jacob's return
to his fond wife after an interview which he has
had with Mme de Vambures. In one sentence Jacob
executes himself: "Plein des mouvements que Mme
de Vambures avait excités dans mon cœur," he says,
"je sautai au cou de mon épouse." Comment is
superfluous.

The critics of the nineteenth and twentieth centuries make a great to-do about the immorality of
Marivaux. Prof. Saintsbury in particular makes merry
with what he considers to be the over-insistence on
the "fair bodie" in *Marianne*. The objection is not
new and arose originally, I think, in the pages of a
journal called *Le Glâneur français* as long ago as
1735. Commenting upon that scene in the *Paysan
parvenu* where Jacob has a rather passionate *tête-
à-tête* with Mme de Ferval, one critic vindicated
Marivaux's right as an artist to reproduce even the

ugliness of life in the interests of truth. The argument is a familiar one, and it will be remembered
was later employed with effect by Flaubert's counsel
in his defence of *Madame Bovary*. The correspondent
of the *Glâneur*, however, explains away the objectionable passage much more plausibly as follows:

> Il (Marivaux) vous avait déjà donné entre un grand nombre
> d'autres portraits, celui de la Coquette, de la Babillarde indiscrète,
> de la Dévote de bonne foi. Il achevait enfin celui de l'Hypocrite et
> pour le finir et vous faire sentir du premier coup d'œil la différence
> d'avec celui de la Demoiselle Habert il lui fallait encore quelques
> traits: c'est à ces derniers coups de maître, qui donnent l'âme du
> tableau, qui en lient toutes les parties et leur prêtent à toutes la
> vie et le mouvement, qu'on reconnaît l'habileté de la main d'où
> ils partent et la beauté du génie de leur auteur.

I have quoted this passage in full for two reasons.
In the first place it indicates, at an early stage in the
evolution of the novel, a precocious understanding of
the aims of the genre, and also of the responsibility
of the novelist. Again, the ingenious explanation of
Marivaux's motives seems to suggest that the author
was trying to accomplish in the novel what Molière
had achieved in comedy, a picture of society made
up of types or *caractères* drawn from various classes.
And indeed this must have been our author's
intention, though his scope was limited by the prevailing moral prejudice against making literature a
reflection of the realities of life.

There is such a thing as relative purity, and Marivaux is, compared to his contemporaries, one of the
least voluptuous writers of the eighteenth century.

His *Marianne* is free from the nastiness of Richardson and the grossness of Fielding, though, as we have seen, certain passages of the *Paysan* invite criticism. At this stage in the evolution of the novel, the novel of manners in particular is about to restrict its observation to a section of fashionable society whose morals have given a quite peculiar connotation to the term "dix-huitième siècle." Before examining the writers of this category, let us consider one last aspect of Marivaux's work.

To what, then, must we attribute his comparative unpopularity as a novelist? It is easy to see why he was not more widely read in his own day: his originality was such as to make contemporaries look at him askance. The first modern critic to appreciate him was La Harpe, who, whilst admiring his skill in handling characters and situations, deplored his *marivaudage*, which he defines thus: "an artifice which consists in clothing subtle and alambicated ideas in popular language, a vicious fluency which leads him to examine one thought from every possible angle and which scarcely ever allows him to leave it till he has spoiled it; in short, a precious and far-fetched neologism which shocks both language and good taste." La Harpe is not alone in his condemnation of Marivaux's peculiar style, and it is difficult to oppose the consensus of critical opinion. The best defence ever offered is that of the author himself: "Chacun a sa façon de s'exprimer qui vient de sa façon de sentir." The difficulty is that there are limits to what language can express, and Marivaux's restless, probing mind is too prone to forget this fact, with the result that he is frequently metaphysical to the point of obscurity. In short, he ignores the truth that what may be a quality in a German philosopher, becomes a positive vice in a French novelist. But again, how few of his readers are fair to him. In the novel of this period we are so accustomed to superficiality, that we do not make the slight mental effort which is necessary in approaching a mind like Marivaux's. This is a pity, because he is one of the eighteenth-century French writers who repays a third reading. In the words of one of his contemporaries, "he grasps nuances of sentiment and passion, and renders palpable, traits which but for him would pass unnoticed." So subtle indeed is his perception that he appears to add to Nature rather than to copy her. Add to this the fact that his two great novels are, technically speaking, unfinished, and we realise why Marivaux has not received his proper place in the history of the evolution of the French novel. His influence on posterity was, however, important, and as we shall see, there is scarcely a modern psychological novelist of note, down to Proust, who is not indebted to him in some particular.

CHAPTER VII

In tracing the evolution of the novel the critic must distinguish between change and progress. It frequently happens, for instance, that a novelist, merely by providing a new and attractive setting for his story, temporarily dazzles the critical eye of the reader and acquires an ephemeral reputation for originality. But Time, that most ruthless of critics, strips away the meretricious covering and reveals the shoddy imposture. This is the history of a species of novel which arose in France about 1734, and which for forty years enjoyed a great vogue. Nor can its popularity be said to have entirely disappeared even now, since one of its chief characteristics is an elegant eroticism which still holds a strong appeal for a certain section of the public that is willing to pay heavily for these "rare and curious" books, as they are somewhat hypocritically described by the Anglo-Saxon book-dealer. I refer to the voluptuous novel of fashionable manners, in a pseudo-oriental setting, whose innovator was Crébillon the younger, the son of the melodramatist and author of *Le Sopha* (1741), which is the archetype of this species of novel.

The astounding success of Galland's translation of

the *Mille et une Nuits* (1704), and of Pétis de la Croix's version of the *Mille et un Jours* (1710), launched a regular cult for the Orient which was reflected in the literature and the decorative arts of France. Playwrights like Lesage and Voltaire vied with the fashionable brothers Martin, the cabinet-makers, in imparting an oriental varnish to their productions. In *Le Bélier* (1730), and in his *Quatre Facardins* (1743), the witty Hamilton set out to ridicule the new fashion, yet so great was the popularity of these charming *contes* that they but added fresh fuel to the conflagration. Scarcely any form of literature escaped the influence. Even the serious Montesquieu capitulated to the oriental vogue, and under the flimsy guise of *Les Lettres persanes* published, in 1721, a scathing criticism of eighteenth-century morals, manners and institutions.

It is said of the elder Crébillon that he regretted having given birth to two things: his *Sémiramis* and his son. The latter's unfilial retort—"Ne vous fâchez pas, mon père, on ne vous attribue ni l'un ni l'autre" —is characteristic, for none can deny the younger Crébillon a certain cynical wit, a sparkling insolence, which detracts attention from the essential shallowness of his work. Like all the novelists of this school, he pursues but one aim, and that is to evoke the applause of the corrupt and *blasé* minority of fashionables who formed what was known in the eighteenth century as *la bonne compagnie*. With a meticulousness certainly worthy of a better cause, and which in the end becomes distressingly monotonous despite the

author's undoubted versatility, Crébillon recounts
the amorous indiscretions of his languorous *marquises*,
his insatiable *duchesses*, and his irresistible *petits-
maîtres*. In his *Ecumoire* (1734), contemporaries
descried beneath the allegory a satire aimed at the
Unigenitus bull, and certain spicy allusions to the
duchesse du Maine and the cardinal de Rohan. But
for the modern reader the chief interest of this novel
lies in its picture—one cannot say its satire—of the
morals of the court. In the *Île Babiole*, to borrow
Crébillon's allegory, love is an obsession. By love
we must understand not a tender sentiment as in
Marivaux, or a tumultuous passion as in Prévost,
but a voluptuous sensation. In this connection it
is difficult to understand why certain critics persist
in referring to Crébillon as a disciple of Marivaux.
He has of course, in some measure, the analytic
manner of Marivaux, but he has that in common
with scores of eighteenth-century French novelists.
On the other hand, Crébillon chooses his characters
from a section of aristocratic society which leads
quite a different life from that of the delightful
people described in *Marianne*. The thinly veiled
viciousness of his women has no counterpart, either,
in the novels of Marivaux, and it is significant that,
in the *Ecumoire*, Crébillon satirises his colleague and
parodies his *marivaudage*. Crébillon's pretty ladies
have a certain disillusioned philosophy which a
character in the *Ecumoire* sums up thus: "L'amant
tendre revient quand la maîtresse sensible disparaît."
To these people coquetry is the life of love, and since

men are not interested in the ordinary manifestations
of a tender passion, it is women's business to call in
art to supplement the shortcomings of nature. Like
Anatole France's Jahel, Crébillon's women are usually
incapable of anything more than a passing physical
attachment, and would agree with the immortal
creator of the abbé Coignard that there is no love
which can resist absence. A similar spirit pervades
Le Sopha, Crébillon's most popular work, which is
based on a conceit borrowed from the doctrine of
metempsychosis. The soul of Amanzée, after many
vicissitudes, is eventually housed in a sofa, and
can only be released if it comes into contact with a
pair of unsophisticated lovers. This ingenious artifice
serves as an excuse for an account of the amours of
a series of society types. It is essentially the procedure
adopted by Lesage in his *Diable boiteux*, though in
other respects the two writers are poles apart. There
is a reminiscence of oriental magic, too, in the short
story called *Le Sylphe* (1730), one of Crébillon's most
graceful efforts which Anatole France certainly remembered when he created his *Rôtisserie de la Reine
Pédauque*.

De Cahusac's *Grigri* (1739) is also an allegorical
novel of manners, but here the setting is pseudo-
Japanese. The court is situated in a blessed isle
whose inhabitants are familiar only with the soft
delights of love, and where conjugal affection is the
height of ridiculousness. The hero of the slender love
story is Grigri, who is looked on as absurd because
he is reasonable. His absurdity is only equalled by

that of the queen, who throws the whole court into consternation by suddenly announcing that she intends to take an hour a day off for thinking. But the real interest is, of course, in the satirical portrait of the perverse artificial society of Versailles. De Cahusac's characters are more ethereally vicious than Crébillon's, and his satirical intention more pronounced. Vice, as he sees it, is more than a matter of physical organisation: it is an attribute of the mind of society. Like our Sterne, he is a master of clever innuendo.

In his preface to *Le Sultan Misapouf* (1746), the abbé de Voisenon cynically informs us that he proposes to make capital of the oriental rage whilst it lasts. "I am convinced," he says, "that the public will soon abandon this unfortunate fashion, and prefer the exaggerated virtue of our former novel heroines to the facility of those who are to be found in modern tales." His avowed intention is to bring matters to a climax by going to the extreme limit permitted by convention. De Voisenon plays upon the metamorphosis idea, and represents Misapouf as having been a fox in some previous incarnation, a theme which provides him with ample opportunity for *double - entendre* of a licentious sort, coupled with an unusual grossness which he apparently borrows from Swift, whose *Gulliver's Travels* he had read in Desfontaines' translation. The worst that can be said of this author is that he carries out the threat held out in his preface. His *Zulmis et Zelmaïde* (1745) is a most amusing and pawky satire of smart society. Monselet once said of La Morlière's *Angola* (1746):

"Dans ce roman est contenu tout le dix-huitième siècle." This is fortunately not literally true. *Angola* is, however, one of the most faithful as well as one of the wittiest pictures of ultra-fashionable society in the eighteenth century. With La Morlière the quasi-oriental setting is of the most diaphanous sort, and admirably enhances the decadence of a world peopled by frail, graceful ladies and elegant, cynical chevaliers. The morbid fear of this society is the fear of mediocrity. To be normal is to be bourgeois, which is a kind of social death. Hence in its language, in its dress, its furniture and its amusements it affects a *bizarrerie* which is the hall‑mark of the *bon ton*. Where La Morlière outstrips his colleagues is in his fidelity to detail. With him the analytic manner is applied, not to psychology, but to *milieu*. It is because of this that he marks a return to the main stream of the novel, for the allegorical, oriental tale is only a backwater. *Angola* has, of course, its fair share of the licence we associate with this type of novel, but it contains a very precise picture of the life of *la bonne compagnie*. Like Gautier, La Morlière might justly have said: "J'étais le peintre de la bande."

Earlier in this chapter I indicated the necessity of distinguishing between change and progress in the novel. In the works we have been discussing, the innovation of the oriental *motif* is not accompanied by any great advance towards a closer approximation to life in such essentials as characterisation and description. Indeed, apart from the somewhat vague picture we derive from the reiteration of amorous adventures, we carry away no precise image of the manners of French eighteenth-century society. The oriental setting marks indeed a retrograde step, for it is but a recrudescence of the *merveilleux* of the seventeenth century in a new and attractive form. It is, in fact, difficult to be original in the licentious novel, as a moment's consideration of the limitations of the theme will show. This has not deterred successive generations from exhausting their talent in a vain attempt to acquire a reputation by following in the footsteps of Crébillon. The latest victim of this illusion is our Mr. Aldous Huxley, whose *Antic Hay* should serve as a warning to his less talented colleagues that the graceful voluptuousness of the French *romanciers corrupteurs* cannot be imitated with impunity by the Anglo-Saxon.

The allegorical novel of manners did not expire with *Angola*. Palissot's *Zelinga* (1749), Chevrier's *Magakou* (1752), Saurin's *Mirza et Fatmé* (1754), are the only three worth mentioning in a long list of others. There is, however, little profit in discussing them, since they present no variants of the type. We may now consider what is, properly speaking, the novel of manners, that is to say the novel unmarred by improbable, oriental elements and which portrays the life of contemporary society. It descends in a direct line from Marivaux and Lesage and, through the latter, from the work of that prince of observers, La Bruyère.

One of the first intimations of the intellectual awakening of eighteenth-century France, is a new curiosity as to the differences which distinguish nations, classes and professions. The spirit of inquiry, which explains the sudden demand for books of travel like those of Tavernier, Chardin and Bernier, accounts also for the new and intense interest in the mode of life of the diverse elements in France itself—the court nobility, the *noblesse de ville*, the provincial aristocracy and the higher bourgeoisie. Following in the wake of playwrights like Dancourt, the novelist begins to study the manners of the Church, the stage, the army, the legal profession and the world of letters. Already, in writers like Scarron and Furetière, we have observed satiric portraits of various social types, portraits which contain, it is true, interesting information as to the life of the time, but in which truth was too often sacrificed for comic effect. To some extent, of course, any objective novelist must reflect the intellectual or material life of his time unless, indeed, like the historical novelist, he deliberately sets out to reproduce the picture of manners of a bygone age. But it is not till we get to the eighteenth century that we find the French novelist reflecting the hundred details regarding the manner in which his contemporaries express their feelings, amuse themselves, eat, dress, house themselves, earn their living—in a word, the hundred ways in which one man differs from another. Trivial in themselves, it is the accumulation of these details that creates the illusion of life, which fascinates us, for instance, in a master like Balzac, whose work represents the highest degree of perfection yet attained in this type of fiction. However, the manners of the reign of Louis XV. are not to be found mirrored in the writings of any individual novelist: they are reflected in an intermittent fashion in about three score obscure novels of the period. Most of these are long since dead and forgotten. As a rule they are badly constructed, and often their style is detestable. Yet, viewed as a body, they do unfold a detailed and vivid picture of upper-class social life in the eighteenth century. The historian cannot afford to ignore them because, though they are all tinged with the mocking satirical note of the period, they combine to form a valuable document on the social life of their day, and illumine corners which the memoirs, journals and correspondence leave in obscurity.

It has already been noted that Lesage is a novelist of manners in the universal sense. For this reason his *Gil Blas* is assured of immortality. The novelists who succeed him, like the journalist, are interested only in actualities; they are topical novelists, careful observers of particular phases of social life, but quite devoid of that Balzacian power of synthesis, that sense of perspective which enables its possessor to view society as a collection of interrelated individuals.

The curiosity of Marivaux, we have seen, is rarely concerned with externals. The examination of the hitherto unexplored recesses of the heart engrosses him almost to the exclusion of everything else. Still, he reveals a Fécour in action, installed at his office desk, and disposing of place-seekers with the studied insolence peculiar to the *arriviste*. Again, Bono is the

first indication in French literature of the presence
of a more civilised financier, a more human and more
generous type in whom avarice has given way to
social ambition. In his *Lettres de Thérèse* (1739),
Bridard de la Garde has left us in his Popino a more
complete example of the genus Bono. We are now
introduced to the financier in his domestic environment, one of those so-called "bonnes maisons"
where there is always a cover laid for the hungry
author who is prepared to pay for his fresh salmon
with a sonnet. Popino is a hedonist whose chief pride
is his *chef*, to whom he pays two hundred pistoles
a year, though his son's tutor is considered over-
salaried at forty. Bridard knows all the tricks of
the profession, the "consular gout," that diplomatic illness which provides immunity from arrest on
settling days, the bogus bankruptcy, the placing of
relatives and *protégés* in the Treasury Department.
His Popino makes Turcaret seem like a mere tyro.

In Campan's *Le Mot et la Chose* we see the financier
of 1750, now almost indistinguishable from the *petit-
maître* whose dress and jargon he sedulously imitates.
By 1760, says the author of *Dorval*, the man of
money is no longer despised by the aristocracy. On
the contrary, he is the arbiter of taste, the Mæcenas
of authors and artists. His wealth is no longer tainted
since his financial operations are sponsored by the
Government. Finance now constitutes a kingdom,
with its princes, its nobility and its third estate.
Unfortunately we are told very little about the
relations between the financiers and the people. De

Mouhy, however, in his *Paysanne parvenue* (1735), draws an excellent picture of a detested *fermier-général* on his country estate. We see him playing the squire in the village church, scolding the beadle for omitting to serve him first at communion, and proceeding pompously to his seigneurial chapel accompanied by a deferential churchwarden.

The attitude of the novelist towards the Church is an interesting one. Marivaux is by no means alone in his accusations of undue influence exercised by the priest in the performance of his duties. Brunet de Brou devotes a whole novel, *La Religieuse malgré elle*, to the question of enforced profession inspired by parental cupidity, a theme which is found in many writers of the time. De Mouhy, in the novel already cited, like Marivaux in his *Marianne*, accuses the convent of venality, and in his *Mémoires d'une Fille de Qualité* asserts that many of the richest nunneries are endowed by girls who have been forced to take the veil. His *Mémoires d'Anne-Marie de Moras* (1740) is based on a contemporary scandal. The lady mentioned in the title was imprisoned in a convent in the rue de Cherche-Midi as a result of her elopement with a Monsieur de Courbon, who was punished by death for his escapade. *La nouvelle Paysanne parvenue* (1744) by G. de la Bataille describes at length the intrigues of conventual politics. If we turn to the secular clergy, we find Fromaget in his *Promenade de Saint-Cloud* (1736) attacking the director of conscience, a favourite character in eighteenth-century fiction. He is here shown in a middle-class home sowing discord between husband and wife. De Mouhy goes farther, and in his *Mémoires d'une Fille de Qualité* portrays a *grand vicaire* who, as trustee of a rich ward, acts as matrimonial agent for a needy but powerful aristocrat. The *abbé petit-maître*, *abbé de cour*, or *abbé commendataire* as he is variously denominated, is an equivocal figure in the social life of the century. He is to be found in every novel of manners of the time. It is but fair to the Church to point out, as many writers do, that these exquisites, though dressed in clericals, have entered into no religious obligations. It must also be mentioned that many of the most virulent attacks against the monastic orders are contained in novels by well-known anti-clerical and propagandist novelists, like Lambert (*Le nouveau Protée* (1740)) and D'Argens (*Le Législateur moderne* (1739)). Generally speaking, however, the Society of Jesus is accused of dangerous and subtle intrigue. Mme Lévesque, a fairly impartial writer, in her *Le Siècle* (1736), openly prefers charges of gross immorality against the regular clergy. On the other hand, the lesser members of the secular clergy, the *curés* of town and country parishes, are ordinarily regarded by the novelist as unintelligent but honest and God-fearing men.

Two novels in particular, *Les Lettres de Thérèse* and Sainte-Colombe's *Les Plaisirs d'un Jour* (1764), give an exhaustive account of stage life. The theatre is the hub of intellectual and social life. The actress is the object of a veritable cult: her dressing-room is frequented by the exquisites of the nobility, of the

Church, the army, law and high finance. Actors perform as best they can amidst a tumult of conversation from the boxes. They are further annoyed by the chatter and movements of the dandies, who occupy seats on the stage itself, an abuse which persisted until 1759. If we add to this the turbulence of the *parterre* and the interruptions of the critics in the amphitheatre, the marvel is that it was possible to preserve the semblance of dramatic illusion. This is a fact which has not been taken into account by critics of the French eighteenth-century theatre, yet it is one which must have had some influence on the technique of playwrights.

Naturally enough, the novelist has little to say about the life of the inner court circle, where of course he had little opportunities for observation. On the other hand, he is well informed as to the doings of the town nobility, which finds the court rather a dull place. Here there is ample evidence of the breaking down of old prejudices and of the beginnings of a class fusion. Marivaux, of course, is one of the first to approach this question of marriage outside the caste. The anonymous author of the *Mémoires du baron de Puineuf* (1737) makes it the theme of his story, and it is generally used because of its obvious romantic possibilities. However, save in rare cases, it is clear that such marriages are entered into solely for financial reasons. But the town nobility mingles with the *roture* chiefly at the green tables, and Chevrier, in his *Colporteur* (1753), exposes the mechanism of a system which employs

needy chevaliers of the Order of Saint - Louis as
croupiers, and enables great ladies to earn large sums
by letting their houses as gambling hells. Others,
like Mme de Pompadour, traffic in clerical benefices,
administrative posts and pensions. The elder sons of
the higher nobility are usually placed in lucrative
army posts. Mauvillon, in his *Soldat parvenu* (1735),
Chevrier in his *Mémoires d'une honnête Femme* (1751),
and Mme Lévesque in *Le Siècle*, have left a damning
indictment of the immorality and arrogance of the
average military officer, but De Mouhy, an ex-cavalry
officer, shows the reverse of the medal when he describes the plight of large numbers of company com-
manders who are passed over in favour of some
court dandy, and who, after forty years' service, find
themselves on the streets with a pension of one
hundred pistoles. But by far the most numerous section of the nobility is the *noblesse de province*. These
country gentlemen, says the author of *Verval* (1753),
are miserably poor and incredibly proud. In many
cases the high-sounding title is derived from some
wretched cottage in some remote province. Extremely
ignorant, they are despised by the rich farmers for
their poverty. Out of a beggarly pittance of eight
hundred francs a year they have to find the money
to purchase a lieutenancy for the eldest son. The
others intrigue for benefices or flock to Paris to swell
the multitude of ambitious and unscrupulous young
fellows, all eager to snatch some junior post in the
army or in the tax-farms. They are the Rastignacs
and Rubemprés of the eighteenth century.

Insincerity, libertinage, the lust for money and publicity—such, according to the novelist, are the characteristic features of polite society. Magny, in his *Spectacles nocturnes* (1756), points to the futility of a literary campaign against this decadence, and makes it clear that novelists who expose certain aspects of society life do so, not with any reformative purpose, but simply because they know that the public demands such pictures of manners. There is still, as has been said, a reminiscence of the satiric tone of the seventeenth - century *romans comiques*. Yet, if one ignores the note of persiflage which is itself but a reflection of the eighteenth - century attitude towards life, one cannot but be impressed by the truthfulness and penetration of these novelists. Compared with other types of fiction which flourished during this period, the didactic, sentimental and moral novels, such works are, numerically, the least considerable. But, from the point of view of the influence they exerted on the development of the novel, they are of great importance, since they keep closer to life than any other. From 1760 until 1830 this type of novel is swamped by the wave of sentimental, moral and subjective fiction, and when it arises again, invested with all the splendour of a *Comédie humaine*, its effect, to say the least, is disconcerting. Critics, following in the track of Brunetière, who did not know these works, explain away the *Comédie humaine* by pointing to the undoubted influence exercised on Balzac by Scott. That Balzac owed him much cannot be gainsaid though he was one of the first to lead the reaction against the *romanesque* manner of treating history. Yet, when his instinct made him break away from this and the absurd imaginings of the Ann Radcliffe school, he was but returning to a field which had been broken in by his own countrymen seventy years before. To indicate this fact is in no way to detract from the originality of Balzac. Is it unreasonable to suppose that he derived some inspiration from these eighteenth - century observers, many of whose novels were reprinted till well into the nineteenth century? Balzac's attitude towards life is largely objective. He is, as Brunetière has pointed out, as positivist in his observation as the philosopher Comte. In this respect both are lineal descendants of the eighteenth-century *philosophes*. The novelists of the reign of Louis XV. tried, not unsuccessfully, to portray the society of their age. One man, Balzac, with his genius, undertook the same task for the society of the Restoration and of Louis Philippe, and succeeded magnificently. He picked up a smouldering torch which, in his hands, burst into bright flames. If we would faithfully trace the development of any form of literature, we cannot afford to ignore the part played by these lesser craftsmen. *Et quasi cursores, vitæ lampada tradunt.*

CHAPTER VIII

THE NOVEL OF PROPAGANDA

IN tracing the development of the French novel, it is not sufficient to indicate that here is a form of literature composed of certain well-defined tendencies all of which reflect some aspect of contemporary life, moral or physical. It is not enough, either, to show that the purpose of the various species of novel is identical with that of the genre as a whole, namely to represent life by relating it with such art as to create in the reader the illusion that he is participating in the existence of the fictitious men and women whose mental and physical adventures are being narrated. The critic or literary historian must also convey the impression of a simultaneous advance of the various elements which he is trying to identify. That is why we are now compelled to retrace our steps and discuss the origins and development of the novel of propaganda, and the novel of sentiment, a knowledge of which is vital to our proper appreciation of the subject of this study. It is no mere truism to affirm that, if we grasp the evolution of the novel at this stage, we shall have moved close to a synthetic conception of the evolution of eighteenth-century French society. Lest this should seem an exaggeration, let the reader consider the extraordinary versatility of this form of literature, even at this stage in its progress. There is hardly a function peculiar to other literary genres which it has not, partially at least, absorbed. The epic, history, tragedy, comedy, satire—all have contributed to feed this insatiable, growing organism. With the advent of Rousseau, lyricism will have to be added to this list. Again, there is scarcely a form of human activity, moral or intellectual, which is not reflected in the novel. The passions and the sentiments of mankind are revealed in the conduct of imaginary men and women, but with a vividness and precision possible only to the novelist, who, unhampered by any law save that of credibility, is able to add to the veracity of the psychological portrait a multitude of picturesque physical traits, and still further captivate our interest by describing the environment of his characters. It would be an over-statement, of course, to claim that the eighteenth-century French novelist had perfected himself in his art, and enough has been said to show that this is far from being the case. There are as yet no Balzacs or Prousts. That fruitful theme of the modern novelist, man's relation to external nature, was barely touched upon, for example, by any French novelist prior to Rousseau. Yet it is clear already, and will, I trust, become abundantly so at the close of this study, that to understand the evolution of the novel is to understand the evolution of manners, morals, sentiments and ideas.

Broadly speaking, there is no novel which does not reflect ideas or ideals, which are simply ideas of perfection. We have noted already in the sixteenth- and seventeenth-century novel the ideas which intellectual society conceived of the perfect life, the perfect lover and the perfect husband. The eighteenth century is above all an age of ideas, all of which tended towards the fulfilment of an ideal relationship between man and his fellow-man: briefly the ideal of a perfect society. Literature becomes the clearing-house for written ideas, just as the *café* and the *salon* become centres where ideas are elaborated and disseminated through the medium of conversation. Certain forms of literature, obviously adapted to the purpose, become the heavily laden vehicles of the new doctrines of political, religious and social reform. Such are the satire, the essay, the pamphlet, the letter, and particularly the newspaper, which, under the inspiration of English models like the *Tatler* and *Spectator*, develops with astonishing rapidity. The *Encyclopedia*, that Juggernaut of the *philosophes*, as the devotees of the new ideas are called, rumbles ponderously towards an unseen morass bearing aloft its Vishnu, an Idea in a wizened human envelope, François Arouet de Voltaire.

Naturally the novel did not escape in the wholesale requisitioning. What more desirable vehicle could be imagined from the point of view of the propagandists eager to broadcast their ideas and theories? The art of propaganda lies in the propagandist's ability to hoodwink his subjects. To the doctor of ideas, the public is the small boy who requires physic in doses of cumulative potency. But the first doses must be administered cautiously and without the knowledge of the patient. The first pills must be sugar-coated, till later the patient, realising the enormous benefit he has obtained, will of his own volition demand his medicine *au naturel*. Such is the theory of propaganda. The novel form in this case supplied the sugar-coating. It remains to be seen whether intellectual propaganda disguised as a novel is, properly speaking, a novel at all.

The practice of using fiction to cloak a more serious purpose than that of merely interesting or amusing the reader is of course very old. The parables and allegories of Eastern literature, the fables of the Ancients, the mediaeval *Roman de la Rose*, the works of the seventeenth-century novelist Camus and others, were essentially didactic productions. It was to instruct his royal pupil, then, that Fénelon, the gentle, mystic bishop of Cambrai, wrote his *Suite du IVe Livre de l'Odyssée ou les Aventures de Télémaque*, published without his consent in 1699. Is *Télémaque* a novel? The question has often been discussed. It formed the subject of a pamphlet in 1736, the author of which refused to consider it as a novel since, he asserted, the purpose of the novel is to amuse and not to instruct. The matter was also taken up in the *Observations sur les Ecrits modernes* (1736), whose editor came to the same conclusion. He looked on *Télémaque* as a sort of prose poem, a new kind of epic, since it introduced moral and philosophic reflections. He refused, however, to grant it the title of novel, chiefly because of the impossibility of the adventures narrated. And even the modern reader, whose conception of the novel has been sufficiently broadened by the influence of Paul Bourget to include the novel with a thesis, cannot dispense with the element of credibility. From this point of view, indeed, *Télémaque* is an anachronism, for even the most improbable of the seventeenth-century heroic fictions managed to free themselves from the *merveilleux*. Strictly speaking, then, *Télémaque* is not a novel, but a hybrid partaking of the novel, the epic, the pastoral and the treatise. It is none the less a classic, and countless little French children since the duc de Bourgogne have followed the mythical wanderings of Telemachus in search of his father, enthralled by the pictures of the dim regions of the underworld and of the smiling Blessed Fields, that happy land where virtuous kings go when they die. Like the hero, they have listened to the sage precepts of their Mentor, and unconsciously imbibed Fénelon's ideas on the perfect state. For this gentle Hellenist who wrote such limpid prose was a political theorist and a courageous reformer. He anticipated most of the changes afterwards advocated by the *philosophes*, though in his ideal state the monarch, who is a sort of benevolent patriarch, is supported by a hierarchy of the upper classes. Fénelon, who realised his responsibility towards France in his office of tutor to her future monarch, insisted that the first duty of a ruler is to govern himself. He must not meddle with religion, or attempt to interfere in private disputes. Whilst controlling legislation, he must leave its administration to his judges. Accessible to all men, he must know human nature so as to avoid becoming the dupe of unscrupulous ministers. It is his duty, above all, to encourage commerce by fostering free trade and agriculture, which is the real strength of a country. The incidence of taxation should be on the lazy and not on the industrious. Speculation should be forbidden, and bankruptcy made a punishable offence. Good workmen must be well paid. The arts and sciences must be encouraged by the wise ruler, who should insist on moderation in dress, in food, and in wine. Fénelon would indeed prefer total prohibition of alcohol, as in La Bétique, that Utopia which Adoam shows to Telemachus. For Fénelon justice and liberty are the foundations of the political edifice, and the rules of morality and politics are identical. *Télémaque* is not the dream of a visionary: it is the *Mene-Tekel* of an enlightened observer whose wise counsels, had they been heeded, might have averted a revolution.

In view of what has been said as to the difficulty of considering *Télémaque* as a novel, some apology is necessary for discussing it in these pages. The explanation is that Fénelon is the pioneer of the eighteenth-century novel of propaganda or, as it is called in its modern form, the *roman à thèse*, which is sometimes quite wrongly rendered in English as "the problem novel." It is interesting to trace the evolution of the thesis novel. Originally, as in the case of *Télé-*

maque, the author is little concerned with the fiction, which is a mere concession to the average reader's frivolous craving for a story. As the novel increases in prestige, however, it becomes evident that this new genre is governed by certain rules which may not be infringed without detriment to art. The reader, trained by a long line of conscientious craftsmen, loses interest in a novel which is a moral treatise with a tale clumsily attached to it. Hence, by a gradual process, the *roman à thèse* evolves in which the propaganda, the plot and the characterisation are so cleverly welded together that the most critical observer can scarcely detect the point of junction. Even then the thesis novel is a dangerous undertaking, and not even an experienced artist like Bourget can always be sure of success, as we see for instance in his *Un Divorce*, which well illustrates the difficulties I have in mind. Plot, characterisation, transcription of time, the interest of suspense are all impeccable, and yet the whole produces an impression of artificiality. It is not representative of real life, and therefore misses that credibility which, as Bourget knows better than anyone, is the essential quality of the good novel.

To return to the eighteenth century, then, we find in the *Lettres persanes* (1721) the attempt of a great publicist and sociologist to write an epistolary novel of propaganda. There is no doubt as to Montesquieu's intentions, and we have only to turn to his *Réflexions sur les Lettres persanes* (1754) to realise his satisfaction at having produced "a species of novel" in

the guise of a collection of letters. He chose to depart
from the old narrative form, for a reason which he
gives in his *Réflexions*. Of epistolary novels he says:
"Novels of this sort are successful usually because
one gives a personal account of one's actual situation,
which makes us feel the passions more vividly than
any recital of them could do." His idea, he then
proceeds to state, is frankly "to join philosophy,
politics and morality to a novel, and to string them
together on a secret invisible thread." This is precisely what he has failed to do, however, and the
romanesque part of the *Lettres persanes* is not inter-
woven with the part that deals with social, religious
and political criticism. The "secret invisible thread"
is not there. It is interesting to note that Montesquieu
is fully conscious of the difficulties that beset the
author of thesis novels. He tells us that he could not
use the historical or the *récit personnel* form, since
his *raisonnements* or arguments would have seemed
improbable, "none of the characters having been
assembled for the purpose of argument, that would
clash with the plan and the nature of the work."
Here is the stumbling-block in all novels which aim
at the dissemination of reformative ideas. Some
credible way must be found in order to fit the propaganda into the action of the novel, and for this
reason, Montesquieu, like so many authors who succeeded him, failed as a novelist. On the other hand,
his views on contemporary society institutions are
penetrating, interesting and sometimes profound.
Montesquieu was no psychologist. He did not under-

stand the sentiments, least of all the sentiment of
love. His proper domain is that of observation and
thought, and here he is in his element. But the chief
objection to the *Lettres persanes*, viewed as a novel,
is its lack of centralised interest. As an epistolary
novel it lacks what Texte called "Une action qui
se reflète tour à tour dans un certain nombre
d'âmes."

What is the plot of the *Lettres persanes*? Stripped
of its digressions, the novel proper reduces itself to
this: Usbek, the master of the harem, is far away. He
receives from time to time letters from his wives
Zachi, Zéphis, Fatmé, Zélis and Roxane, in which
they assure him of their love and growing despair
at his prolonged absence. Their protestations and
plaints are mingled with a certain amount of "family"
gossip. But soon Usbek learns from his head eunuch
that all is not well. It is increasingly evident that
there is a growing spirit of unrest and revolt among
the wives, and this culminates in the discovery of a
man in the harem. Soon all the wives but Roxane
are openly insubordinate. Usbek is furious, and orders
his eunuch to restore discipline at whatever cost.
The grand eunuch is murdered, whereupon his suc-
cessor, Solim, gets instructions to purify the seraglio.
The lustration is ruthlessly carried out despite the
protests of the ladies, who live in a reign of terror.
Suddenly it is found that the immaculate Roxane,
the flower of the flock, has been unfaithful. Her lover
whom she had smuggled into the harem, stabs Solim
and is condemned to death. The last letter is from

Roxane to Usbek. Before committing suicide, she confesses cynically that she has gloried in deceiving a hated tyrant who, having bought her body, imagined fondly that he had purchased her soul, her self-respect and her freedom.

It will be observed that there is not sufficient central action, and that there are no adventures, either physical or psychological, leading up to the *dénouement*. Montesquieu had intended to paint the growing sexual irritation (*la fureur*) of the wives and the gradual waning of their love owing to the absence and indifference of Usbek. But so impotent is he as a psychologist, so deficient is he in creative imagination that, instead of a series of analytical portraits, of intimate confessions, all we get is a picture unpleasantly suggestive of the disorder in a *maison close* in the absence of the chief bully.

Montesquieu was very proud that his *Lettres* preceded Mme de Grafigny's *Lettres péruviennes* and Richardson's *Letters of Pamela*. In fact, he is the innovator of this form of the novel, though we have seen that his theories were badly carried into practice. The letter form of the novel was the natural outcome of the seventeenth-century fondness for such collections as *Cent Lettres d'Amour écrites d'Evandre à Cléante* (1646), *Le Roman des Lettres* (1667), and of course the celebrated *Lettres d'une Religieuse portugaise* (1668), which gave rise to many imitations. None of these works, however, are so definitely in the novel form as the *Lettres persanes*, which popularised this new species before the translation of

Richardson's *Pamela* in 1742. It was the Englishman, nevertheless, who showed by his successful handling of the form what were its real possibilities. On the other hand, Montesquieu's subordination of plot and characterisation to his penchant for reflections and critical observations tended to retard the development of the epistolary novel in France, since his imitators exaggerated the defect and produced collections of letters which were not novels at all.

Like most young men of his time, Montesquieu was attracted by the prevailing vogue for the Orient, and the harem *motif* in his *Lettres* connects him with the *romanciers corrupteurs* Crébillon, La Morlière and others. None of his critics have regretted this aspect of his work more keenly than the author himself, but it was undoubtedly these descriptions of badgered eunuchs and restless *odalisques* which first appealed to the overheated imagination of the Regency public. Rather illogically, we think only of the Montesquieu of the *Esprit des Lois*, the germ of which is in the *Lettres*, and we forget that he was only thirty-two when he produced his earlier work, and thus his oriental indiscretions strike us as incongruous and somewhat shocking. In reality they occupy a negligible place in the book, and prove nothing against their author save that he was human enough to be of his century.

The idea, which has since become very common, of making a foreigner the mouthpiece of the author's criticism of his country was not original even in 1721. Marana's *L'Espion du grand Seigneur* (1684),

Dufresny's *Amusements sérieux et critiques* (1699), and at least two other works, employed the same useful device before Montesquieu. Usbek, the serious reflective Persian, deals with graver subjects like religion, divorce and suicide. Rica, on the contrary, is Montesquieu in lighter, satiric vein. It is he who brilliantly reviews the passing show—literature, modes, street-types, *cafés*, *salons*, women. For Montesquieu is that rare phenomenon, a thoughtful journalist, and the *Lettres persanes*, apart from the harem *motif*, is an arsenal of ideas, sometimes profound, but more often only suggestive, a sort of French *Spectator*. However, these pages are more than a gallery of Regency society types. In addition to the squibs, there is a quantity of explosive material, for Montesquieu undermines the foundations of religion and of the *grand monarque* legend. The king is a great magician who can persuade his people that one crown is worth two, and that a piece of paper is money. So great is his power that he can convince his subjects that he has the gift of healing by touch. Yet, observes the ingenuous Rica, he is not so great a magician as the Pope, who can make one believe that three are one, that bread is not bread, and wine is not wine. Usbek is astonished at the inconsistencies of Louis XIV. He has a minister of eighteen and a mistress of eighty; he loves religion, yet cannot suffer those who say it should be rigorously observed; he loves victories yet is afraid to have a good general. Such is the tone of the *Lettres*; destructive, irreligious, critical, this work is the opportune expression of a national state of mind. It crystallises the sceptical ideas of the Regency.

Imitation is the criterion of success in literature, but it is rare, as Voltaire remarked, to find an imitation which shows how the original ought to have been written. This is sadly true of the mass of productions evoked by the fame of the *Lettres persanes*. Purporting to be written by Chinese, Jews, Iroquois and Peruvians, all these letters contain satires levelled at religion, or at the political institutions of the century. Few, however, even pretend to assume the novel form. Saint-Foix's *Lettres turques* (1730) is a typical example. There is little attempt to follow up the destiny of the heroine, Rosalide, who flees to France from Turkey with a French count, Mazaro, who had once been a slave in Constantinople. From Paris Rosalide writes to her sister Fatima, a contented inmate of the harem of Bostangi Bacha. Saint-Foix gives a detailed picture of the manners of high society, and criticises abuses like gambling, the cynical immorality of conjugal life, and the barbarous custom of forcing young girls to take the veil, in order to keep the inheritance intact for the eldest son. Fatima's letters veil the deistic propaganda already familiar to the French since the beginning of the century, through the writings of Saint-Evremond and the *libertins*. In an intercalated story, *L'Histoire de Félime et d'Abderamen*, the anti-clerical thesis is even more vigorously sustained. Saint-Foix outlines a plan for the limitation of recruiting in the monastic orders, which he considers a menace to the economic welfare of France. He proposes that the "Bonzes, Faquirs and Derviches" should be mulcted to provide pensions for deserving officers, and that no one should be allowed to take holy orders without first having engaged in some trade or profession for at least ten years. In this way the king will enjoy the services of some ten thousand citizens who annually dedicate themselves to a life of uselessness. The same hatred of the clergy forms the subject of D'Argen's *Le Législateur moderne* (1739), and it is interesting to note in both these works that the anti-clericalism is largely a reflection of caste prejudice, the contempt and hatred of the impecunious aristocrat for the monks—that "collection of wretches sprung for the most part from the dregs of the people."

Mme de Grafigny's *Lettres péruviennes* (1747) was immensely popular. Like Montesquieu, this author was keenly alive to the importance of probability in the novel. She makes an attempt to preserve local colour by introducing Peruvian names and customs into the love story which forms the backbone of the action. Zilia, a Peruvian, is in love with her countryman Aza, who is in Spain. Déterville, a young Frenchman, is hopelessly infatuated with his exotic *protégée*. The faithless Aza is converted to Catholicism and marries a Spaniard. Déterville joins the celibate order of Malta. Zilia, realising that she can never love again, retires to the quiet of her country estate and devotes her life to study. She is a feminist, a *femme philosophe*, but her feminism does not exclude an exquisite sensibility. We know enough of the unfortunate life of Mme de Grafigny to realise that Zilia is a discreet portrait of the authoress.

Her criticism of contemporary French society is peculiarly interesting because it is free from the flippant, satiric tone of the male novelists we have discussed. Grafigny is convinced that the prevailing attitude towards women is merely a passing mode. However, she holds the man entirely responsible for the laxness of feminine morality. The adulterous wife, she maintains, is the product of a social condition where any display of marital affection is evidence of a defect in breeding. The Frenchwoman is the victim of a stupid system of education which, as Mme de Grafigny puts it, is "a masterpiece of inconsequence." The object of the system is to prepare woman for society life, and she is therefore enclosed in a convent and taught by nuns, who have naturally little knowledge of the world and are generally most unintelligent! Again, while she is taught that honour consists in having no lovers, all her training is directed towards pleasing the other sex. The law connives at the subjection of woman by affording the wife no redress against a brutal husband who dissipates her dowry with his mistresses. The young girl can be forced to take the veil by ambitious parents who desire thus to favour their sons. Girls never learn the true meaning of humanity, even in its simplest form—kindness towards servants. The absence of reciprocity in marriage and in love hardens some women, and makes others stupid and fatuous. In all classes of society

woman is downtrodden. The only difference is that
the woman of the people becomes a beast of burden,
while the society woman is betrayed and insulted.
It is refreshing to read the eloquent indictment of
a sensible woman like Mme de Grafigny: it is a wholesome antidote to the graceful, smiling picture drawn
by Voltaire of—

> ces belles contrées
> Où d'un peuple poli les femmes adorées
> Reçoivent cet encens que l'on doit à vos yeux;
> Compagnes d'un époux et reines en tous lieux,
> Libres sans déshonneur et sages sans contrainte.

But though these lines were, unfortunately, not
generally applicable, there was, as Mme de Grafigny
admits, a minority of intelligent women who, like
Zilia, found a refuge from masculine injustice in
science and the arts. *Les Lettres péruviennes* is one
of the first feminist novels, and its author the predecessor of modern writers like Paul Margueritte and
Bourget. Incidentally, Mme de Grafigny is perhaps
the only novelist prior to Rousseau to evince any
real appreciation for the poetry and the grandeur of
external nature. Again, her moral tone is significant.
Here is a writer who conceives woman not merely as
a creature of passion and sensibility, but as a reasonable being endowed with intelligent curiosity, and
capable of other sentiments than those of love. We
shall see this conception of woman take strong hold
of the novel, and it will be no surprise to find feminine
France hail with delight the novels of the feminist
Richardson. Mme de Grafigny, then, paves the way

for the moral school of novelists who flourished
during the last forty years of the eighteenth century.
Voltaire's views on novels and novelists are well
known. He was even more contemptuous of them
than Montesquieu, and never seems to have realised
that the novel was developing into a powerful and
independent genre. In 1733 he expressed his satisfaction at the apparent decay of fiction, which he
thought the public had abandoned for history. By
1746, however, he saw that the taste for novels, far
from abating, was rapidly growing. With the oppor-
tunism of the true propagandist, he realised that
here was an excellent outlet for his subversive ideas,
and from 1746 until 1775 poured forth a stream of
fiction in the shape of *contes*, novels and dialogues.
It is true that he dubbed all these productions *romans*,
but in the strict technical sense only two deserve
the name. Academically speaking, of course, the *conte*
is a sub-species of the novel, with its own technique,
but its evolution is so bound up with that of the
novel, that any attempt to treat it separately at this
stage would but lead to confusion. The main characteristic of the *conte* is the obvious improbability of
its adventures, situations and characters. We saw, in
discussing the erotic novelists, pictures of manners
disguised as *contes*, and in the eighteenth century, if
we except the *contes de fées*, it will be found that
most of the fictions called *contes* are really short
novels. Sometimes, as in Voltaire, the fantastic or
marvellous trappings are preserved, or, as in the case
of Marmontel, there is no trace of them.

Voltaire's fictions bear the same resemblance to novels as the marionette show does to a real play. His Zadig, Candide, Cunégonde and Pangloss are puppets and not characters. They have adventures and they speak and act; but always we are conscious that the voice is that of Voltaire who directs their every movement with his magic fingers. But the reader is not seriously concerned with their individual fate. Their love affairs evoke no sympathy. We watch their antics and listen to their conversation, because of the sheer delight of hearing Voltaire's raillery, and of seeing monuments of stupidity and superstition crumble under the deadly barrage of his logic. What an exquisite instrument is the Voltairean phrase! Who will undertake to define Voltaire's wit? His narrative style is superb. We forget the sheer improbability of the adventures in our amazement at the art of the narrator, who can pass without the slightest effort from a parody of the flowery oriental tale, as in *Zadig* (1747), to the picaresque, *Gil Blas* manner of *Candide* (1759), or astonish us with the Richardsonian pathos of the *Histoire de Jenni* (1775). Is this the same Voltaire, we ask ourselves as we read the last-named work with its closely argued refutation of atheism, its defence of the doctrine of immortality, and of the immanent justice and goodness of God? It is Voltaire, but Voltaire at his finest. The old savage hatred of intolerance still flashes out, the old detestation of superstition flares up. "L'athée est un homme d'esprit qui se trompe; le superstitieux est un sot brutal qui n'a jamais eu que les idées des

autres." The mellowness of age has brought with it
a calmer, more patient attitude towards the world.
The author of *Babouc* (1746), of *Zadig* and of *Memnon*
(1750), like Kipling's butterfly, preached contentment
to the toads beneath the harrow. Life was good to
Voltaire then. He has no illusions about its imper-
fections; but on the whole it is a passable place.
Better leave it alone. Live in moderation and abandon
the reforming of this madhouse we call the universe
to fanatics and fools. *Micromégas* (1752) reveals
a change. Voltaire is bitterly disappointed with
Frederick and all the other sedentary barbarians who
control the destinies of human beings, and, "digesting
their dinner in the comfort of their study, issue
orders for the massacre of a million men, then go
out to offer up solemn thanks to God." The world
is an absurd heap of mud, swarming with excited
homunculi, whose antics appear ridiculous when
we conceive their littleness in the universal order
of things. *Candide* (1759) is undoubtedly Voltaire's
masterpiece. The luckless hero and his Cunégonde,
with Pangloss the Leibnitzian optimist, are plunged
from one misfortune into another. Outraged, robbed,
cheated, beaten, and nearly killed by the inhabitants
of this "best of all possible worlds," they arrive, in
the last chapter, at the conclusion that the happy
man is he who quietly "cultivates his garden." The
world is full of misery and injustice. To move about
in it is to invite trouble: so the wise man will keep
still within his four walls.

L'Ingénu (1756) is more hopeful. It is an attack

on religion and fanaticism. L'Ingénu is the simple Huron who falls a victim to the Christian craze for converting people who already possess a perfectly good religion of their own. Voltaire, in passing, satirises the Crown's persecution of the Huguenots, indicts the Jesuits for hypocrisy and immorality, and arraigns the whole administrative system on charges of corruption, tyranny and imbecility. He implies, however, that men are not impervious to reason, since even a blackguard like his Saint-Ponange and an obstinate Jansenist like Gordon can be shown the error of their ways. Voltaire's optimism increases with his age. He was eighty-one when he wrote the *Histoire de Jenni*, which closes on a note of benevolent resignation. The world is a place of horror and confusion. At its two poles stand atheism and fanaticism, but between them lies a zone of virtue. Here man may find happiness. "Walk firmly along this path," is his exhortation. "Believe in a good God and be good." Moderation, the practice of humanity, belief in the justice of God, such are the chief articles of Voltaire's philosophic creed. They carry, of course, the implication that the world is sadly imperfect, and that man is more prone to error than to right-doing, since he refuses to obey the dictates of a wise Providence, who has endowed him with reason for this purpose. That is why superficial students of these novels have rushed to the conclusion that Voltaire is a pessimist. The reply to this fallacy is that he is no more a pessimist than a fervid Christian like Pascal. On the contrary, he is an optimist, since he believes in the saving grace of reason. He is an optimist without illusions.

Long before the eighteenth century we find, in France as in other countries, satirical writings directed against the regular clergy. The *fabliaux* and *contes* of the Middle Ages and of the fifteenth century are full of malicious references to the alleged immoralities of the various monastic orders. We have seen also, in Scarron and Sorel, a continuation of this current which runs through the French novel till the Revolution. It was not, however, until the beginning of the eighteenth century that the novelist instituted serious and violent propaganda against the convent viewed as a menace to society, selecting as his chief target the question of enforced profession. Brunet de Brou, in his *Religieuse malgré elle* (1720), devoted a whole novel to the story of a girl who, as usual, was forced to take the vows in order to satisfy the unnatural demands of her parents, who in this way assured to their son the undivided possession of their succession. Other novelists, like D'Argens, De Mouhy and Marivaux, emphasised the evil results of this system, and accused the convents of complicity inspired by material motives. That such cases were rare is shown by the publicity accorded to certain revealed examples of the abuse, but it is easy to see the romanesque possibilities latent in such situations of enforced vocation, and to realise what a powerful weapon they afforded the *philosophes* in their anti-clerical activities.

In the case of Diderot's *La Religieuse*, however, there can be no question of influence exercised by this novel on the public sentiment of the eighteenth century, for though it was composed in 1760, it was not published until 1796.

It is interesting, nevertheless, as a reflection of the spirit of its time, and above all as an example of the consummate powers of persuasion with which a great novelist can endow his art when he subordinates it to purposes of social reform. Diderot's master-stroke was to represent the heroine as desiring to break her vows solely because the religious vocation was repugnant to her reason, and not, as was the case in other novels of this type, for motives of a purely sentimental sort. Again, Diderot was too much of a realist not to realise the fundamental impro-bability, or at least the exceptional nature, of the stock motive imputed to parental harshness, namely the materialistic one. He assumed, therefore, that the victim, Suzanne Simonin, was a natural child, and thus explained very plausibly the hatred of M. Simonin, who suspects her illegitimacy. The unnatural conduct of the mother he attributed to remorse and the very probable desire to get rid of a child who daily reminds her not only of her error, but of the cruelty of Suzanne's real father.

Suzanne's noviciate is a happy period, during which the mother-superior, by feigned sympathy and every possible indulgence, tries to surmount her novice's objections to the vocation. The fatal day arrives and, to the general consternation, the heroine publicly refuses to take the vows. She is taken home, and after a period of solitary confinement is informed by her confessor of her actual position in the family. In the moral conflict which ensues between filial love and reason, Diderot attains a pitch of dramatic realism which places him above Richardson. Suzanne's capitulation appears absolutely inevitable, since we realise that, owing to the economic dependence of woman in the social order of the century, there is virtually no alternative.

In describing Suzanne's experiences under a series of mother-superiors, Diderot exposes a picture calculated to inflame the most torpid imagination. The keynote of the novel is persecution enhanced by the elements of mystery and fiendish cruelty such as we find in the popular, melodramatic novels of the early nineteenth century. But Diderot's realism is uncannily convincing. Like Richardson, he slowly accumulates apparently insignificant details, till the illusion of reality can finally no longer be denied. The essential appeal of all work of this sort, I think, is the intolerable suggestion that these unnameable horrors are taking place within a few yards of the ordinary, happy bustle of the workaday world, and that, between Suzanne and the righteous justice which an outraged society would mete out to her persecutors, there is a sinister barrier of impenetrable hypocrisy, lies and misrepresentations.

The very prejudice of society against nuns works in favour of the persecutors, since, as Diderot insinuates, the law fears that, to facilitate the renunciation of vows would lead to a flood of requests like Suzanne's. In his gallery of types of superiors, he presents a

series of psychological studies of abnormalities produced by the unhealthy atmosphere of the convent
quietism, exalted superstition, fanatic, sadistic cruelty
and repression culminating in sexual mania. It is
perhaps just as well that this novel was not published
until after the promulgation of the decree suppressing
the religious orders, since it would almost certainly
have led to an outbreak of violence and arson.

It will have been observed that almost the only
setting as yet not borrowed from the legitimate novel
by the propagandist is the historical one. Marmontel's
Bélisaire (1767), however, is situated in the reign of
Justinian, a period sufficiently remote, one would have
thought, not to offend the susceptibilities of anyone.
Yet one chapter made its author a European figure.
The story is incredibly dull. Bélisaire, a successful
general and popular hero, is falsely accused by his
enemies of plotting against Justinian. The emperor,
persuaded by his consort Theodora, orders Bélisaire's
imprisonment. The people clamour for his release,
and he is set free, but only after having been blinded.
His wife dies. Tiberius, the son of Justinian, admires
Bélisaire's virtue and wisdom, and arranges a meeting
between his father and the patriarch. Justinian sees
Bélisaire incognito and is filled with remorse. The
rest of the book consists of conversations on virtue
and government. One of these is contained in the
notorious chapter which deals with civil intolerance.
Marmontel maintained the view that the monarch
had no right to lend military aid to any one sect in
order to persecute nonconformists. A man's religious

beliefs are his private concern. This argument, to-day a mere commonplace, aroused a storm of protest from the Church. After a noisy polemical battle, the Sorbonne formally censured the book in 1767. Meanwhile it had been translated into several languages, and Catherine of Russia, and the kings of Sweden and Poland, had written to congratulate the author. Letters poured in from all sides, even from far-off Carolina. Marmontel's victory over the *sorbonniqueurs*, as Voltaire called them, was complete. *Bélisaire* has no longer anything but an historical interest for us. It was a courageous blow dealt for liberty of thought, but, like all novels of propaganda, bore within it the seeds of its own destruction. This type of novel, and the modern *roman à thèse*, are ephemeral productions, for once the object for which they were written is attained, they have no further reason for existing. However, they will probably continue to appear till the arrival of the millennium, or the death of the novel as a genre. From the artistic point of view they will always be unsatisfactory, because they are at variance with the essential purpose of the novel, which is to offer a credible picture of life, and not to preach sermons or to disseminate propaganda.

CHAPTER IX

THE GROWTH OF SENSIBILITY

THERE are few tender heroines in the French novel of the seventeenth century. Facetious contemporaries like Boileau made fun of the *grands pleurards* portrayed by Scudéry, but the studied *galanterie* of the lovers in these heroic novels is without a vestige of true sensibility. The celebrated *Carte de Tendre* itself, despite its misleading name, is a striking testimonial to the complete lack of real sentiment in the novel of that period. Sensibility is not a characteristic of aristocratic literature, and it would be difficult to point to a more classic example of such a literature than the heroic novel of the age of Louis XIV. Examine any of the "portraits" which abound in Scudéry's fictions — that of Arricide in *Clélie*, for instance. One finds a detailed catalogue of intellectual and moral qualities, together with a list of carefully recorded traits composing the physiognomy of the subject: one looks in vain, however, for any evidence of a soul. As for the satirical novels of Scarron, Sorel and Furetière, we not only discover a complete absence of sensibility, but an absolute insensitiveness to situations which ordinarily arouse pity or humanity. It is for this reason that the letters of the Portuguese nun surprise us with the precocious sadness of their melody, so oddly out of tune with the spirit of their times.

When the French novel, under the influence of tragedy, essayed a true picture of the movements of the soul, it naturally concentrated, not on the gentler sentiments, but on the passions. That is why the *Princesse de Clèves* and *Manon Lescaut* are short novels. Like tragedy, they waste no time on preliminaries. They do not, as they might well do, trace the dawning of love and analyse the conflicting sentiments which are usually the prelude to the explosion of a great passion. Mme de Lafayette and Prévost are still of the seventeenth century in this regard: they are concerned, not with sensibility, but with passion, and above all with the tragic conflict between reason and passion. Prévost is not, however, consistent in this respect, but Mme de Lafayette is, and in all her novels the characters are either reasonable or passionate. They are never merely sentimental. Marmontel, at the close of the eighteenth century, could refer to the *Princesse de Clèves* as a dangerous book and, according to the moral-utilitarian standards of his day, he was right, for Mme de Clèves is *une âme d'élite*. Had she possessed the sensibility of the average woman, instead of the exceptional strength of mind which was hers, she would have slipped over the precipice. After all, in real life it is excess of sensibility or pity, as the novelist calls it, and not passion which commonly produces complications in woman's life. Yet, prior to the eighteenth century, the French novelist hardly exploited this theme, a curious fact which may perhaps be explained by the repressive influence of convention and education. Heroines were either colourless, passive agents or reasonable, highly principled beings swept away by a sudden passion, too often without any other reason than the assumption that everyone was bound to have a grand passion, as everyone in the seventeenth century had smallpox—at least once in a lifetime. The one weakness of the *Princesse de Clèves*, indeed, is connected with this very assumption. Why, we ask ourselves, does a woman of the intelligence and culture of Mme de Clèves fall passionately in love with a peacock like Nemours? The motivation in *Manon* is much more plausible. The physical beauty of Manon and her wistful helplessness sufficiently explain the infatuation of the impetuous chevalier, for Manon is a typical example of the passive heroine already referred to. One can understand simplism in the dramatist of the seventeenth century, though it is indeed a sign of bad art. He had to concentrate on salient psychological features in the exposition of characters, and was of course further restricted by his so-called unities of time, place and action. Novelists have no such excuse, yet we have seen that, at the end of the seventeenth century in particular, the writers of the Lafayette school modelled their work on tragedy. By doing so they imposed upon themselves unnecessary restrictions, because they did not yet realise the possibilities latent in the new genre, the novel. That is why Marivaux's rôle in the evolution of the novel is so important since, by his minute analytic procedure, he showed that love is not necessarily always a torturing passion. Besides revealing the nuances of the sentiments in the spectrum of love, he discovered also that people can harbour interesting and exquisite emotions without being in the slightest degree amorous. Marianne is a subtle blend of sensitiveness and sensibility. Her extraordinary self-consciousness is not entirely due to the amour-propre of the coquette, but to the sensibility of a mind which craves happiness, though not at the expense of others. The exquisite consideration which moves her to conceal her delight in her own beauty so as not to humiliate the ill-favoured servant-girl, Toinon, is a new note in the French novel. The same sensibility makes her forget to be a coquette when she sees her lover in church: it accentuates the pathos of her loneliness, and twists through the fabric of the novel like a warm and glinting thread of gold. Marianne's character is indeed a curious blend of natural sensibility and acquired egotism. In happier circumstances, one feels she would have been entirely swayed by sentiment, but her poverty, her loneliness and experience of the world have somewhat hardened her. We cannot forget that Marivaux frequented the *salon* of Mme de Lambert, who wrote in her *Réflexions nouvelles sur les Femmes*: "You can have neither humanity nor generosity without sensibility. A single sentiment, a single movement of the heart means more to the soul than all the maxims of the philosophers." And what is the theme of Marianne but a plea for sensibility which reaches its climax in the scene where Mme de Miran flouts interest, reason and convention by consenting to the marriage of her son with a penniless little nobody, whose pathetic situation and whose generosity and delicacy touch a responsive chord in her own susceptible heart. Marivaux accurately described this work as "l'histoire du cœur dans les conditions médiocres," for the nuances of emotion which he lays bare have no place in the aristocratic literature which preceded *Marianne*. Again, if we examine his other great novel, we cannot but see that the one redeeming feature of Jacob's unlovely character is its flashes of disinterested sympathy. He assists Mlle Habert, the maiden lady who is overcome by faintness on the Pont Neuf, and out of gratitude she marries him. He has nothing to gain by renouncing a good position in favour of M. Dorville, or by dashing to the rescue of a stranger attacked by armed men. If his generosity brings him fortune, then we must infer with the author that sensibility carries its own reward.

We have noted the intense melancholy and craving for sympathy of Prévost's heroes, but often their sensibility is exaggerated self-pity. Prévost is a classic, and in all his work the dominant note is the clash between reason and passion. For his characters life is one prolonged crisis, and that explains his love for the melodramatic and the *macabre*, for, if he is to keep his heroes in a state of tragic suspense, their adventures must be correspondingly dramatic. His characters are so consistently unfortunate, that we feel it would be unreasonable to expect them to display sensibility for the misfortunes of others. They are all children on whom life has never smiled. Yet they possess a kind of universalised sensibility. Like the later Romantics, they are filled with a longing to take all mankind to their heart. They are philanthropists, humanitarians, philosophers and moralists. Prévost is the father of the moral novel of the second half of the century, and his *Mémoires d'un honnête Homme* (1745) announce Marmontel, Rousseau and Saint-Pierre just as surely as his earlier works explain the sombre, melodramatic elements in the sentimental novels of Baculard d'Arnaud.

It is natural to look to the feminine novelists for evidence of sensibility in the early French novels of the eighteenth century, and we find it in Mme de Tencin's *Comte de Comminge* (1735). It is said that no one is quite so sentimental as the confirmed libertine, and the example of this renegade nun, who wrote so touchingly of the misfortunes of lovers, lends colour to the generalisation. This is a tale of two lovers separated by the enmity of parents. The count is another Des Grieux, but his passion is tempered with a sensibility unknown to Prévost's heroes. Adélaïde, the heroine, is also a *cœur sensible*, but with all the moral courage of a Mme de Clèves. She is not afraid to reveal her sentiments to her lover, but there is never any hesitation as to her course of conduct. The count pleads with her to go away with him to some "corner of the world" where they can hide their identity and live for themselves alone, but

Adélaïde's reply is that ill-fortune can only be defeated by constancy and virtue. In a word, she has no Romantic illusions. In Comminge we have already the pre-Romantic hero, who seeks in nature a fitting setting for his melancholy, and his sensibility drives him to the Pyrenees, where, amid rugged mountains, foaming torrents and mournful cypresses, he finds a delicious added sadness. Adélaïde, in an ecstasy of self-sacrifice, marries a brutal country nobleman in order to secure the release of her lover, who has been imprisoned by a harsh father. Like Prévost, Mme de Tencin delights in the ultra-romanesque. Comminge, disguised as an architect, procures a meeting with his beloved, whose husband he wounds in a duel. Filled with remorse, he flees and hears that Adélaïde is dead. Comminge then becomes a Trappist monk. Some years later the tolling of the funeral bell calls him to the death-bed of a young novice, who confesses that she is Adélaïde, who had been shut up in a tower by her husband. After his death, "un mouvement inconnu" drew her to the convent, where, disguised as a monk, she had lived for some years, so as to be near her unsuspecting lover. The final scene is highly pathetic and the heroine expires in the arms of her lover, whilst tears run down the cheeks of the tender Trappists. Comminge becomes a hermit. This novel ushers in the era of sensibility in French fiction. Read by thousands, it was reprinted all through the eighteenth century. Baculard d'Arnaud dramatised it, and wrote another novel of the same name, which also enjoyed enormous success.

It is clear that a new type of lover is evolving in the novel. Love, as conceived by the new school, is no longer a passion, but a tender sentiment which inspires its victims with a sweet melancholy. Mme Lambert summed up the ideals of the new movement when she wrote: "Qui dit amoureux dit triste." It is the eighteenth-century reaction against the licence of the Regency and of the court of young Louis XV. An élite of tender, melancholy souls opposes the pleasures of virtuous, hopeless love to the cynical, refined sensuality of the worldlings. Love, says Mme Lambert, is a union of hearts, a secret penchant which is understood by the true lover, though it may not be expressed. Real love "desires little, hopes for little, and asks for nothing." If her ideals had prevailed, it is easy to see what would have been the result, for it was she who suggested that a school should be established to cultivate the soul, and to purify love by bringing it closer to the Platonic conception. Fortunately the novels of Prévost and of Mme de Tencin counteracted the preciosity of some of Mme Lambert's doctrines, which sublimated the sentiments to the point of improbability.

At this stage we are forcibly reminded of similar tendencies which were revealing themselves in the novels of the Englishman Richardson, whose *Pamela*, *Clarissa*, and to a lesser degree *Grandison*, were later to exercise a profound influence on the French mind. However, we may for the moment postpone discussion of these, and examine certain native novels which preceded the appearance of the French translation of *Pamela*, first rendered into French by Prévost in 1742. It has been claimed by the latter's biographer, Harisse, that this novel would not have appealed to the French in literal translation, but a comparison of the two books reveals no essential differences, save here and there the paraphrase of a sentence which would have sounded ridiculous in a word-for-word rendering. We shall see, indeed, that there was little to surprise Gallic readers of *Pamela*, either in the sentiments expressed or in the situations which were exposed. The main theme, that of innocence persecuted by vice, was certainly not novel, and Prévost's *Cleveland* and the *Mémoires d'un Homme de Qualité* contain several illustrations of this idea. One remembers, too, the attempts made on Marianne's chastity by Climal, which have led hasty critics to conjecture that Richardson imitated Marivaux. But there is no actual similarity between the Tartuffian Climal and the brutal, stupid, would-be seducer Mr. B. This type of villain appears in several French novels prior to 1742, thus anticipating not only the scoundrelly persecutor of Pamela, but the more refined and cynical Lovelace.

In Crébillon's *Egarements du Cœur et de l'Esprit* (1736), Marivaux's analytic method is applied, not to the sentiments, but to the sensations aroused by love. The comte de Versac, who obviously recalls Molière's *Don Juan*, corrupts the young hero and attempts in vain to pursue the virtuous Mlle de Théville. In Duclos' *Histoire de Mme de Luz* (1741), the wicked judge Thurin forces the unhappy heroine to purchase

with her honour certain documents which incriminate
her husband. She is later drugged and violated by
her director of conscience, the perfidious Hardouin.
In the same author's *Les Confessions du comte de * *
(1742), Mme de Selves is deserted by her seducer,
but by her Pamela-like sweetness and resignation
she succeeds in converting him from his evil ways,
and finds happiness in that "union of hearts which
is the fruit and the principle of virtue." Nouvelle
de Montador's *Confessions de la comtesse de * * (1744),
admittedly inspired by Duclos' book, is a long recital
of misfortunes and persecutions, beside which even
Clarissa's trials seem quite insignificant. Clearly, then,
the French were prepared for Richardson's tales of
persecuted virtue, and even had their novels not
paved the way, the "whining comedies" of the La
Chaussée school would have done so.

Nevertheless, the triumph of morality in the French
novel over other elements was consummated by the
popularity of Richardson's *Pamela* and *Clarissa*.
Crébillon and Duclos dwell with perverse satisfaction on the voluptuous aspect of their theme. They
deliberately appeal to the senses, and one cannot take
seriously their pathetic descriptions of the victims'
grief. In this respect they are much more the predecessors of Rousseau and Laclos than is Richardson,
who is too vulgarly or brutally realistic to be morally
harmful. Prévost and Tencin are absolutely moral in
their intentions. Marivaux is more suspect, but he is
saved from immorality by his natural good taste
and his predilection for the analysis of the more

delicate sentiments associated with love. He is the Watteau of the novel, as Richardson is its Greuze.

A common tendency is evident in two species of French novels in the early part of the eighteenth century, both of which merge in the sentimental, moral tale so popular from the fifties to the Revolution. Both species are preoccupied with the theme of the wronged but virtuous woman. The first springs really from the tragic novel of the Lafayette school. In the *Princesse de Clèves*, the lover Nemours has a very secondary rôle, but a few strokes of the pen would suffice to convert him from a coxcomb and philanderer into a libertine and seducer, like Lovelace or Laclos' Valmont of the *Liaisons dangereuses*. Prévost's Gelin, in *Cleveland*, represents the extreme limit to which this type may be pushed, and he is of course too melodramatic to be probable. The prevailing tone of this school is highly moral, and usually the heroine is unfortunate through no fault of her own. In the other class of novel of this sort, the woman is generally as active as the man. She is a coquette who plays with fire, so that her ultimate fate does not arouse that pathos which we associate with the unfortunate woman in Prévost or Duclos. The marquise de M—— in Crébillon's *Lettres de la marquise de M—— au comte de R——* (1732) is an excellent example of the second type. She is an *allumeuse* who plays with the count, a highly sophisticated Marianne in fact, but a frail Marianne who is finally caught in a net of her own weaving. Jealousy is her undoing; that, and too much sensibility. "Ah!

je n'ai que trop de sensibilité," she cries, "mais
l'amour n'est que cela!" Like Flaubert's Madame
Bovary, she is deserted and commits suicide. The
same author, in his *Egarements*, gives us in Mme de
Lursan a new character, the woman of forty with a
past, which she has lived down by years of exemplary
conduct. She meets a young man, the son of a very
dear friend. Soon she realises that he is aware of her
history and is physically attracted by her. Although
in love, she repulses his advances, but finally, rather
than see him the prey of a society woman of evil
repute, Mme de Lursan determines to satisfy what is
at the same time the last caprice and the first real
passion of her life. In novels of this sort great emphasis
is laid on the picture of contemporary society morals.
In this respect they are novels of manners, though
they are rarely concerned with the *milieu* in which
society moves. They preserve the seventeenth-century
contempt for details, which concern the "furnishings"
of the novel—*le costume*, as Fénelon calls it. They
continue one aspect of Marivaux's analytic procedure,
which they apply in particular to physical love, and
in general confine their observations to the *bon ton*.
Yet, as we have seen, they prepare the minds of their
readers for the *Clarissa* type of fiction, just as surely
as does Prévost. It is interesting to watch in Crébillon
the fluctuations of two tendencies. Before he definitely
abandons himself to the erotic novel of the *Sopha*
type, he reveals in his *Lettres de la marquise de * **
a blend of sensuality and sensibility in which we can
easily see an exaggerated reflection of Marivaux.

Later, when he realised that the consensus of public opinion condemned the licence of his *contes*, he definitely identified himself with the new movement in his *Heureux orphelins* (1754), and in his highly moral *Lettres de la duchesse de * * * (1768).

Before the arrival of Richardson then, various tendencies dispute for mastery in the French novel. Prévost, continuing the tragic school of Lafayette, drifts into melodrama. Yet by his intransigent morality and his keen sensibility, he anticipates English influence. By his deism and humanitarianism he joins hands with the propagandist novelists. Marivaux is unwittingly responsible for the voluptuous novel, which flourished under various disguises, but affected, in particular, an oriental costume. In another direction he gives rise to a school of novelists of manners, many of whom, like De Mouhy, enhance their pictures of society with recitals of melodramatic adventures *à la* Prévost. Crébillon and Duclos try to compromise between voluptuousness and sensibility. Obviously some strong directive force was necessary to produce order in this chaos of conflicting elements. It came from Richardson, the creator, in England, of the moral and sentimental novel, and for many years a household name in French literary circles. What was the precise scope of the influence exerted on the French novel by the gifted author of *Clarissa*? In a brilliant study on literary cosmopolitanism published some thirty years ago, Joseph Texte answered this question by setting up Richardson as an innovator who moulded the destinies of

the French novel till the Revolution. We have already
seen that this conception of Richardson is an exaggerated one, and is in fact due to Texte's imperfect knowledge of the previous history of the French
novel. In any case the question is sufficiently interesting to justify a fresh scrutiny of *Pamela* and *Clarissa*,
together with the chief works of such French novelists
as are popularly supposed to have modelled themselves on the two English classics.

In the *Letters of Pamela* Richardson recounts the
improbable martyrdom of a fifteen-year-old serving-
wench who, in a series of letters to her parents eked
out by the author's explanatory interpolations, unfolds a harrowing tale of attempted seduction by her
master, a Mr. B., whose character, such as it is—for
he is a shadowy figure,—is that of a conceited and
sensual country boor. Pamela, on the other hand,
has brains, or, if you like, a kind of peasant's shrewd-
ness, coupled with an immeasurable opinion of her
own importance. Through two interminable volumes
she harps on her virtue, yet, with the dreadful per-
tinacity of the fanatic, persists in exposing herself
to the continued onslaughts of Mr. B., although on
several occasions there was apparently nothing to
prevent her returning to her parents. The latter, by
the way, had warned her to be on her guard before
there was the slightest grounds for misgivings. There
is, however, one obstacle to her leaving: it is her
secret admiration for the lout who ill-uses her. It
is possible that Richardson intended to depict the
dawnings of love in a virginal mind. The picture

which he actually presents is the enjoyable self-abasement of a woman of the people, who glories in being brutalised by the stronger sex. It is easy to see why Pamela appealed to the English reading public of the eighteenth century, for it has all the elements of melodrama combined with the spiciness of the choicer sections of the *Newgate Calendar*. The sub-title is *Virtue rewarded*: "Perseverance repaid" would be more appropriate for, despite all the plausible moralisings of Richardson, the practical lesson which he imparts is, not to shun temptation, but to hold out till virtue can be bartered for a wedding-ring. This is of course sound advice, and it is what passes for morality or chastity in certain strata of society to-day, though usually it is inculcated with a frankness which is preferable at least to Richardsonian cant. Writers like Fielding in England, and in France Villaret and Mauvillon, retorted with "Anti-Pamelas." So much has been made of the success of *Pamela* in France, that it is just as well to note that there was a reverse to the medal. Des Bois, a collaborator of Prévost's, remarked in 1742 that the French public objected to the fiddle-faddle which drowned that simplicity and *naïveté* which constituted the sole merit of the book in question. The sardonic writer of a *Lettre sur Paméla* (1742) waxed facetious on the conduct of Pamela, that "connaisseuse en œillades," and the numerous attempts upon her virtue, each of which is duly followed by "une vapeur d'honneur qui la fait tomber en syncope." I mention these facts, not because they detract essentially from Richardson's popularity, but to show the persistence of that realistic, mocking Gallic spirit which has so frequently preserved French literature from the worst excesses of sentimentality and over-idealism. In England *Pamela* gave rise to a number of what the critic of the *Monthly Review* (1752) called "kitchen novels": it did not do so in France, and indeed, despite fairly diligent research, I have not been able to discover a single novel of even third-rate rank in French which is modelled upon *Pamela*, or which could not have been written had *Pamela* never existed.

Richardson's real fame in France was due to his *Clarissa*, whose heroine is of a social condition less calculated to shock the prejudices of eighteenth-century Frenchmen. The story is so well known that a bare outline will serve our purpose. Goaded by the harshness of her family, Clarissa, rather than marry the stupid Solmes, elopes with the libertine Lovelace, who lures her to a disorderly house, where she is drugged and abused. The harrowing tale of her mental and physical sufferings ends with her death and that of the villain, who expiates his crime in an agony of remorse. He is killed in a duel by Clarissa's virtuous cousin Morden. The hard-hearted parents, the reformed scoundrel, the drugging episode, were already familiar *clichés* to French readers of Tencin, Prévost and Duclos. But in both *Pamela* and *Clarissa* there was another element which was bound to appeal to the French, just because perhaps it was not new to them. I refer to the artistic suspense which precedes the seduction in *Clarissa* and which, in *Pamela*, leads not to a seduction, but to a highly improbable conversion of the villain. Crébillon and Duclos practised this method with great success, the former in a frankly salacious manner, the latter with insincere moral pretensions. It is the method of the popular novelist, although Richardson, by his exceptional fidelity to psychological truth, his attention to detail, and his dramatic sense, rises above the class of novel immortalised by the late Mrs. Henry Wood, the French counterpart of which is called the *roman feuilleton*. Prévost, who translated *Clarissa* in 1751, did Richardson an inestimable service. By his own novels, he had already accustomed the French to such tales of persecuted innocence, but, as his friend Des Bois warned him, the effect of these stories, which made little impression on the English mind, was such as to make a Frenchman shudder. It was probably with this in view that Prévost "chastised," as he said, the language of *Clarissa*, and excised the gruesome details concerning the death and funeral. Richardson was of course furious, but he need not have been, since not till 1772 did the anglomaniac Suard consider it advisable to try the French public with the omitted passages, which he translated in the *Journal étranger*. Even then, he addressed himself rather apologetically to those readers whose hearts were not too weak to stand "a succession of profound and strong emotions." We can understand his diffidence better if we hastily review the progress which sensibility had made in French literature generally up to this point.

We have noted the inroads made by sensibility in the novel. The same spirit was reflected even more clearly in the theatre, where, under the influence of Destouches and La Chaussée, a new type of play, the so-called *comédie larmoyante*, was evolved. We know from Bridard de la Garde's *Lettres de Thérèse* what a doubtful reception was at first accorded by fashionable society to this new genre. These sentimental and very moral dramas kept many fair heads assiduously bent over their netting-needles, for it was as yet "bad form" to weep at the theatre. But soon the public flocked to La Chaussée's *Mélanide* (1741), and despite the ironical remarks of some critics, wept with Bridard at these lachrymose plays, which he hailed as the "most precious discovery ever made in the empire of the Muses." The *bon ton* followed suit because, as Mme Puisieux insinuates, it was the fashion. "Les femmes prennent des ridicules comme des modes," she says. "Il y a des temps où il est du bel air d'avoir des vapeurs" (1750). For the mass of the nation, however, it was more than a passing mode. A moral and sentimental revolution was in progress. There were many who felt like poor, brave Vauvenargues, that the age of reason had failed to produce a virtuous, happy society, and that the fundamental goodness which is in man could only be liberated by an appeal to his sentiment. Vauvenargues' own life, brief as it was, served as an exemplar of his doctrines. Contemplating it, a Voltaire could cry with rare sincerity: "Had you been born but a few years earlier, my works would have been better!"

The *larmoyant* genre claimed Voltaire too, for, in spite of his early scoffings, he produced an *Enfant prodigue* (1736) and a *Nanine* (1749). In a word, the atmosphere of France was surcharged with sentimental and moral elements, and the country was prepared to welcome the doctrines of Richardson. *Clarissa*, in the "chastised" version, struck a sympathetic chord which reverberated through the French novel for half a century. *Grandison*, on the contrary, needed all the prestige of its author to impose itself on the French public. I cannot agree with Texte, that its morality appeared sublime, nor with his general thesis that Richardson revolutionised the French novel, by converting it from a frivolous and romanesque production into a serious genre capable of supporting moral ideas. One cannot completely ignore the serious, moral trend of the latter seventeenth-century feminine school, which, we must recollect, imitated neo-classic tragedy and specialised in such themes as the virtue of renunciation and the moral conflict between passion and duty. There has been a strong tendency, also, to overlook the debt which the French novel owes to Prévost, who, despite his penchant for melodrama, had a remarkable sense of his responsibility as a writer and disseminator of moral truths. The inclination has been to confuse Richardson's services to the English novel, where he was indeed an innovator, with his extraordinary popularity in France, where his rôle was not so much that of innovator, but of director, whose timely arrival gave stimulus and new life to a species of

novel which for years had been slowly emerging from
a number of amorphous elements. The essential link
between Richardson and the French writers of the
new movement was their common conception of the
purpose of the novel, which they now envisaged as
a medium for the inculcation of moral truths. In
France, at least, this substitution of an ethical for
an æsthetic standard was not confined to the art
of the novelist. The wearisome, but highly moral
dramas of Diderot, Sedaine and Mercier, the detestable poetry of Saint-Lambert and Delille, and the
didactic, sentimental pictures of Greuze, indicate all
too plainly the literary and artistic taste of the period.
Yet in the novel it is difficult to point to evidence
of direct imitation of Richardson. Sometimes, in works
by obscure and bad writers, we come across titles
obviously suggested by *Pamela* and *Clarissa* and
Grandison. French heroes and heroines appear with
English names; scenes are laid in an English setting
by authors who had obviously never crossed the
Channel; a type of Englishman is evolved who
appears in all the French novels of the second half
of the century, the generous, melancholy philosopher
with suicidal tendencies—a type familiar to readers
of Prévost. He is the eighteenth-century counterpart of the modern "stage Frenchman." Again, the
critic must guard against the temptation to draw
facile conclusions, from the masses of novels which
bear the label "traduits de l'anglais," large numbers
of which are bogus translations, as a very hasty
perusal of the critical notices of the *Monthly Review*

will show. It is significant, however, that the French
public demanded novels dressed up *à l'anglaise*,
though it would be risky, we have seen, to infer
that these works were English in substance. Many
novelists, as Texte points out, invoked the name
of Richardson, which was held in almost general
reverence. Also, most writers tried as far as possible
to impart an English colour to their novels, whilst
of course the letter form popularised by the famous
Englishman was widely adopted. All this, however,
throws no light on the fundamental question of the
real influence alleged to have been exercised by
Richardson on the art of the French novelist. In
this connection it will perhaps be worth while to
glance at the content of some novels which were
extremely popular in France after 1742; that is, after
the appearance of Richardson in France.

CHAPTER X

THE French cult for Richardson was merely one aspect of that anglomania which, as Buckle once pointed out, is the most immense fact in the history of European thought in the eighteenth century. With many novelists it assumed the form of intellectual snobbery, and it was for such writers a great source of comfort to be able to acclaim one of their number as a *penseur*. It is not surprising, then, to find real thinkers like Voltaire reluctant to join in the general rejoicing which Dorat, himself a novelist as well as a poet, expressed in the following outburst: "O Fénelon! O Richardson! You are but novelists, and posterity will place you beside the greatest poets!" The *Idées sur les Romans* containing these words were published in 1771, but since they summarise views which admirers of Richardson had been expressing for twenty years, we may reproduce them at this point. There is in the English character, says Dorat, a "vigorous sap" which flows into all their writings. The English novelists depict man as he is in nature. They seize the avenues which lead straight to the soul, and "catch passion in the act" whilst the French but express it by reminiscence. Some-

173

times, it is true, they are accused of paying too much attention to detail, but is not that the secret of their genius? The English writer has the gift of observation, and, in studying man, he neglects not the smallest particular, for he knows, says Dorat,—and here he anticipates Balzac—that "the physical exterior is the torch which reveals the inner man: the contraction of a muscle is the key to a sentiment." Dorat is keenly alive to the importance of the apparently superficial details which Richardson records so carefully. "They serve to prepare the way for the supreme effort, and to graduate the impressions." The English method, he thinks, is to mine patiently before producing the great explosion: the French dissipate their energies in a series of brilliant pyrotechnic displays. A novel, to be a work of art, must be of moral utility, and if the novelist is to surprise the secret of nature, he must prepare his mind by "profound meditation and solitary contemplation." His soul must be charged with enthusiasm for good, and with that melancholy whose august imprint may be discerned on all the ideas which emanate from it. It is clear that Dorat appreciates the essential qualities of Richardson's work and his *Idées*, though they lack the fire of Diderot's celebrated eulogy, express at least a critical judgment. But when, after reading these observations, we turn to the novel of which they are the preface, what is our astonishment to find not a single trace of English influence. The work, as we shall see in due course, is thoroughly French in inspiration and in composition. Dorat omitted one important aspect of Richardson's originality, which his colleague, La Dixmérie, however, is careful to emphasise. After referring to *Pamela, Clarissa* and *Grandison* as "courses in practical morality," the latter goes on to say in his *Discours sur l'Origine, le Progrès et le Genre des Romans* (1773): "In them we see actors of every condition; that is to say, no rank is despised—a source of interest which is all the more effective since it brings the majority of readers into close touch with the characters who must attract them. This is a secret which our French novelists have too long overlooked or despised." Now, thanks to the progress of reason, observes La Dixmérie, "the times and the point of view have changed. We now know that there are men in all classes of society, no single one of which holds a monopoly of virtue."

Contemporary France, then, was critically alive to the chief qualities of Richardson's genius—his respect for moral and psychological truth, his democratic conception of society, and above all the art underlying his slow cumulative procedure, whereby he gradually prepares the way for his crises, holding the reader in a state of suspense, and at the same time reflecting not only the facts of existence, but also the slow passage of time which, in real life, inevitably surrounds these facts. With these things in mind, let us now turn to the popular novelists who, in France, began to write after the advent of Richardson.

It would be difficult to point to a writer more representative of the prevailing French taste in fiction than Baculard d'Arnaud, who, for some forty years, ravaged the sensibilities of the public with his sentimental, moral and unspeakably morbid tales. Fréron, the editor of the *Année littéraire*, in which, by the way, D'Arnaud had a financial interest, compared him to Fénelon and Massillon, and suggested even that his works should be used by the Government for educational purposes. However, apart from other reasons, when Fréron discusses sentimental, moral and other anti-philosophic productions, his judgment is not to be trusted. La Harpe is nearer the truth when he says briefly that D'Arnaud's novels are saturated with prolix declamation. Baculard's first novel, *L'Epoux malheureux* (1745), is a mild example of his manner, and was suggested to its author by the unfortunate experience of a certain M. and Mme de la Bedoyère. The hero marries an actress, and is disinherited and relentlessly pursued by his parents, who procure annulment of the marriage. Like Prévost, whom he constantly imitates, Baculard plunges his victims into misfortune after misfortune. Time and again happiness is within their grasp. All is forgiven, but at the crucial moment the tender-hearted friend who is watching their interests suddenly appears, urging them to flee. The events are hopelessly improbable; there is absolutely no psychological truth in the character-portrayal, yet the novel was eagerly read for its morality and exaggerated pathos. "Sensibility," declaims the hero, "is the true life; it is sensibility which makes us realise the value of existence, and the emotions which it procures to the soul necessarily beget virtues and good actions." Such is also the tone of Baculard's celebrated *Epreuves du Sentiment* (1772–81), where for five mortal volumes the author employs every device known to bad fiction in order to wring the hearts of his readers. Base seducers, weeping victims, white-haired old fathers, faithful retainers, jealous rivals, orphans, poverty-stricken widows, secret marriages, big-hearted seigneurs and judges—the list is an endless one. Baculard, not content with mere pathos, claimed to have invented *le genre sombre*, which, of course, was Prévost's speciality, and grave-yard meditations *à la* Young drew fresh floods from the already overworked tear-ducts of the lovers of sensibility. D'Arnaud preaches the doctrine of a return to nature and, like Rousseau, regards the social conventions as the source of the misfortunes of the true *cœur sensible*, which revolts against the sensuality and artificiality of society. Like Richardson, whom he occasionally recalls, he is democratic in his general outlook, and it is in the humbler ranks that he finds the most shining examples of virtue. But Baculard is really a disciple of Prévost, the cosmopolitan, and many of his heroes are, like Cleveland's, "les plus malheureux des hommes." In general men are "ferocious beasts," preying on the misfortunes of their fellows. However, this does not daunt the *cœur sensible*, who derives a certain delicious satisfaction from injustice. These pre-Romantics form a chosen tribe, drawn from every nation and united by the common bond of humanity. National prejudices, politics and war, which are the barbarous products of society, do not exist for Baculard's heroes. "They recognise a common country, a common origin and a common family." In D'Arnaud we can trace the steady growth of individualism, of cosmopolitanism, of dawning Romanticism, and of that belief in the predominance of sentiment over reason which Rousseau and his school opposed to the rationalistic doctrines of the *philosophes*.

The hero of Prévost's *Mémoires d'un honnête Homme* (1745) really anticipates Grandison, for he is the pattern of all the virtues and an insufferable moraliser. Prévost delights in placing his hero in equivocal situations, which afford him an opportunity of behaving like a true *philosophe*. A lady with whom his father is in love throws herself at his head, and the *honnête homme*, who has fallen in love elsewhere, is faced with a delicate case of conscience, which gives rise to lengthy moralisings. His inamorata turns out to be a married woman: hence a little discourse on the sanctity of marriage. An actress, the mistress of a friend, pursues the harassed hero, who philosophises on the sacredness of friendship. Various incidents are dragged in to show the magnanimity, the philanthropy and the superhuman perfection of this paragon, who appears in various disguises in different novels of the second half of the century. We find him in D'Argen's *Solitaire Philosophe* (1736), in the anonymous *Guerrier Philosophe* (1744) and *Le Philosophe amoureux* (1746), in Chamberlan's *Le Philosophe malgré lui*, etc. Prévost's last novel, *Le Monde moral* (1760), is in the same vein. It is really a series of loosely connected

and extraordinary incidents, which the author examines with a view to probing the motives of the
principal actors. Prévost's psychological explanations,
however, are as bizarre as the events described, and
but for some interesting side-lights on the private
life of the poor country nobility, the novel would be
utterly worthless.

I mentioned that Richardson's *Grandison* is reminiscent of the *Honnête Homme*. One of the most
interesting problems in *Grandison* is the conflict
between love and religious duty, a fruitful theme
not, however, touched upon by Prévost, and unex-
ploited in French literature until the appearance of
Voltaire's *Zaïre* in 1732. It was of course this play
which suggested to Godard d'Aucour the subject of
his *Mémoires turcs* (1753), where Atalide, a Christian
slave in the harem of a very civilised, eighteenth-
century Turk, renounces her love in order to take
the veil. D'Aucour's novel is otherwise interesting
as a link between the plaintive letters of the *Religieuse portugaise* and the lyric passion of the *Nouvelle
Héloïse*. But where Richardson was able to portray
the mental sufferings of a Protestant and a Roman
Catholic, Godard d'Aucour, like Voltaire, deemed it
wiser to picture the conflict in the hearts of a Christian
and a Mohammedan. Apart from the fear of censorship, he had other reasons. The romantic history of
Mlle Aïssé, the beautiful Circassian slave, and her
touching love affair with the chevalier D'Ayde were
still "good copy," whilst curiosity as to Turkish
manners was at its height. Besides, it is doubtful

whether the matrimonial problems of a Protestant and Roman Catholic would have had the same romantic appeal to lovers of sensibility.

Equally popular on both sides of the Channel, Mme Riccoboni, the unhappy wife of the celebrated playwright, reflected in her novels not a little of her own disillusionment and sensibility. She is very French in her subtle analysis of love, which occupies an exclusive place in the minds of her characters. But though in this respect she is a disciple of Marivaux and the younger Crébillon, there is a poignancy in her descriptions and a lack of restraint which remind us of the author of *Manon*. She usually affects the letter form, and in the titles of her *Lettres de Mistress Fanni Butler* (1757) and of *Les Lettres de Mylady Catesby* (1759), as also in the local colour, there is a superficial reminiscence of Richardson. Apart from this, however, there is no echo of the immortal *Clarissa* in these novels. Mylady Catesby is a typical Riccoboni heroine, the innocent victim of male injustice, for one of the favourite devices of this author is to erect a barrier of inexplicable reticence between her lovers. Catesby, for example, suffers unspeakable anguish when her lover suddenly leaves her to marry a certain Jenny Montfort. The key to the enigma is that the hero, D'Ossery, in a drunken frolic, had compromised Jenny, and like an *honnête homme* married her. Consumption, that popular novelist's malady, extricates Mme Riccoboni from an awkward situation, and Mylady Catesby, who has a tender heart, forgives, marries and forgets.

The *Histoire du marquis de Cressy* (1758) is a powerful work, because of the chief character Cressy, who reminds us at once of Versac and Lovelace. After winning the love of Adélaïde de Bujei, Cressy, with whom a rich young widow, Mme Raisel, is infatuated, marries the latter partly from vanity, partly from mercenary motives, and to some extent because he is attracted by her beauty. Mme Riccoboni has portrayed in Adélaïde a pathetic example of the ravages of sensibility in a too tender heart. Stunned by her desertion, Adélaïde goes to a convent and writes to Cressy. Mme Raisel, who has not been told the whole truth, is puzzled at the reproachful tone of the letter. Cressy, meanwhile, is carrying on an intrigue with a *protégée* of his wife's, Hortense Berneuil, who is living with them. The cold, sensual and capricious nature of Hortense is an excellent study, and her jealousy at Cressy's reconciliation with his wife is most convincingly described. The "obligatory scene," the interview between Mme de Cressy and Adélaïde, is highly dramatic.

Probably Mme Riccoboni had *Clarissa* in mind when she wrote the final chapter, in which Mme de Cressy, on hearing from a rival that she has been again betrayed, quietly prepares to commit suicide. This final scene, where she tells her husband that she is speaking to him for the last time, is described with restrained intensity and with a complete absence of melodrama. There are no Richardsonian moralisings, though the agony of Cressy's remorse is every whit as dramatic as Lovelace's. Cressy is a completely changed man. He becomes powerful, distinguished and respected, but, says the author simply, "il ne fut point heureux." I think this is a more artistic ending than Richardson's, and more probable. It is not in accord with the Englishman's Old Testament ideas on punishment, and here Mme Riccoboni sharply differs from the stern morality of the sentimental school, for whom death was the proper penalty to be meted out to evil-doers.

The *Histoire de Miss Jenny* (1762), in the manner of D'Arnaud, is disappointing. A bogus marriage is the excuse for a deluge of false pathos and maudlin, improbable remorse. Mme Riccoboni recovers her old powers, however, in the *Lettres de la comtesse de Sancerre* (1766). Here the letter form interferes with the action of the novel, as it is nearly always apt to do, owing to the constant necessity for repetition. Mme Riccoboni analyses the changing emotions in the mind of a widow, Mme de Sancerre, who is in love with a distressingly perfect married man, Montalais, whose chief defect is a too close resemblance to Grandison. Mme de Sancerre is the first interesting widow in French fiction, because she is neither funny nor immoral. To her friends she is a source of mystery, because she abandoned her husband, afterwards killed in battle, and, while he lived, a model husband. The most interesting part of the novel is the explanation of this enigma, for Mme de Sancerre confides to a friend the true facts of her married life, which reveal the extraordinary character of the late Sancerre. It transpires that Mme de Sancerre's uncle, to protect

his niece, had made it a condition of the marriage
that, in the event of misconduct on the part of Sancerre, his money would go to the wife. Sancerre's
character is a peculiar combination of sensuality,
hypocrisy and cruelty. His wife surprises a passionate
intrigue and has, unknown to her husband, retained
one letter—the proof of his infamy. Her temptation
to use the letter is very great, but her natural delicacy
and sensibility will not allow her to do so. Finally,
goaded by ill-treatment, she reveals to her husband
that she holds this weapon and insists upon separa-
tion. On her husband's death she is filled with immense
relief, and acquires a reputation for insensibility. In
reality she is profoundly emotional, but her experience
has inspired her with a distrust of all men. Her love
for Montalais is a source of torture. Again and again
she resolves to go away, but always some indispensable
reason for remaining presents itself. Even on the
death of Montalais' wife happiness seems as far off
as ever, because he does not speak. Here we have a
situation reminiscent of Marivaux. There is no longer
any outside obstacle to their love, but Mme de Sancerre cannot precipitate the *dénouement* while Montalais is intimidated by her apparent indifference and
hauteur. At last he confesses that his reticence is due
to her fortune, and all ends happily. It will be seen,
then, that Mme Riccoboni represents the persistence
of the pure French tradition, and that, when she goes
outside her own temperament for inspiration, it is to
Marivaux and Crébillon, and perhaps Prévost, that
she turns and only to a slight extent to Richardson.

Mme Riccoboni has been called a feminist, and indeed most of her heroines are the patient, silent victims of masculine caprice and cruelty. But the judgment is rather a superficial one. Men are, of course, deceivers, but that is part of their nature, just as it is women's to forgive. There is little trace of the advocate of women's rights in the novels of Mme Riccoboni. She does not, like Mme Grafigny, inveigh against the social system which educates woman with the sole object of making her an instrument of man's selfishness. In her *Histoire d'Ernestine* (177?), indeed, there is an implied criticism of feminism, in the conception of the character of the heroine's friend Henriette, who is an artist and a modern woman. Henriette, discovering that Ernestine is unconsciously living on the bounty of the marquis de Clémengis, accuses the latter of wicked designs, and has to apologise on finding that the marquis is a high-souled philanthropist who is prevented from disclosing his love by the uncertainty as to the outcome of a lawsuit, on which depend his fortune and social freedom.

In 1755 there began to appear in the *Mercure* a series of short stories by Marmontel, a friend of Voltaire, and of course an enemy of J.–J. Rousseau, who unwittingly offended Marmontel by sending him a gift copy of one of his books with the ambiguous dedication: "Non pas à l'auteur du *Mercure* mais à M. de Marmontel." These early *contes* were intended as criticisms of certain social foibles which had escaped the comic authors. Destouches, in his *L'Ingrat*, *Le Glorieux* and *Le Médisant*, pale counterfeits of

Molière's type comedies, had prepared the way for
the moral and sentimental drama. Marmontel, in
his *contes*, helped to foster a similar spirit in the
novel, but it was not till 1758 that he broke away
from the indulgent cynicism of his original manner,
which smacks strongly of *Le Sopha* and *Zadig*. Yet
even at this stage one can detect the didactic note,
for Marmontel rarely wrote unless he had what some
American critics are fond of calling "a message."
In *Alcibiade*, for instance, his "message" is for the
rich young man who is naïve enough to believe that
he can be loved for himself alone. *Bélise* is for the
romantic young woman who pines for life as it
is pictured in fiction. Cécile, the widow in *Tout ou
Rien*, realises the folly of pandering to the whims of
a jealous lover. *Le Philosophe soi-disant* is a really
amusing satire on the faddist who poses as a philosopher. It is not difficult to detect in the hero Ariste
a malicious parody of Rousseau, who is represented
as a boorish fellow affecting in his speech and dress
a profound disdain for the social amenities, a pro-
fessed vegetarian who devours meat greedily under
protest, enlarges on the corruption of society and
the "doux instincts de la nature," yet, alas! falls
into a carefully baited trap set by a shrewd and
wealthy old *présidente*.

These *Mercure* tales were collected and published
in book form by Marmontel in 1761, under the
significant title of *Contes moraux*. Their success was
enormous, and the author's fame spread to England,
Italy and Germany. An enlarged edition appeared in

1765, to be followed by many others. Ten well-known writers, including La Dixmérie, and that dreadful pedant Mme de Genlis, produced *Contes moraux*, but the imitations, though widely read, are much inferior to the originals. The morality of Marmontel's stories is what appeals least to us to-day, though eighteenth-century readers savoured it with delight. As to the structure of the *contes*, we can agree with the author when he confesses that his *dénouements* are frequently hurried and improbable. His chief weakness is a lack of that precision, movement and finish which ought to distinguish writings of this sort. But the absence of these characteristics in Marmontel is a logical result of his initial error, his attempt to inflict on the *conte* a burden which it was never designed to carry. The atrabilious Fréron was therefore quite right when he remarked: "Il est plus aisé de faire des contes moraux que des contes intéressants."

Marmontel paved the way in France for a domestic novel of the sort so brilliantly represented in England by Fielding and Richardson. Yet love plays a surprisingly small part in his tales, which are largely concerned with social and family problems. He defended the solidarity of the home against the inroads of an individualism which in society circles masqueraded as tolerance. His *Bonne Mère* is a sharp condemnation of the "passez-moi la rhubarbe et je vous passerai le séné" type of *ménage*, and here he has the austerity of the English outlook which is to-day reflected in writers like Bourget and Bordeaux. Again, many novelists had discussed the theme of filial duty: Marmontel was, however, the first to emphasise the question of parental responsibility. In the *Mauvaise Mère* he attacked a very common abuse, the preference usually shown to the eldest son at the expense of the other children, and in the *Ecole des Pères* he reveals what may happen in a family where the son is shielded by a too fond mother and neglected by a wealthy and busy father. In the *Bon Mari* a serious, virtuous man struggles with the problem of domesticating a frivolous wife who has advanced ideas on the question of feminine liberty. Thanks to the advice of officious friends, the wife comes to regard herself as a champion of women's rights, and the family is threatened with destruction, but at the eleventh hour husband and wife are brought together by their common love for their children. Marmontel has a strong fund of common sense, which distinguishes him from the ruck of sentimental and melodramatic novelists like D'Arnaud and Mercier, who also imitated his moral tales. Indeed, in the *Heureux Divorce*, he pokes fun at the conventional heroine who longs for the "délices des âmes et les charmes des cœurs passionnés." And an original and welcome note is sounded in the *Femme comme il y en a peu*, where Marmontel portrays a new type of wronged woman. Acélie, married to an amiable and fickle spendthrift, Mélidor, discovers that her husband is not only deeply in debt, but is entangled with a *cocotte* Eléonore, who, abetted by a false friend of Mélidor's, is quietly feathering her nest at the expense of her lover. Ignoring her husband's wounded amour-propre, Acélie compounds with Eléonore, silences the usurer, and settles with the creditors. This practical and strong-minded lady then proceeds to evolve a system of education for her children (she has obviously read the second part of *Pamela*), and having, like Marmontel, frequented the society of the physiocrats, organises the exploitation of her husband's estates, with the help of a council of seven wise villagers.

Marmontel's sensibility finds expression in a sort of practical humanitarianism. A peasant himself, though he rose outside his class, he is filled with pity for the patience and suffering of the lower classes. "The people are good, docile, officious and honest," he says in the *Misanthrope corrigé*, where he exposes his ideas on rural improvement. Like all the *philosophes*, he is anti-revolutionary, and his reforms are directed, not at the prevailing institutions, but at abuses in the administration of these institutions. He looks to the *seigneur* to protect his peasants against the rapacity of the tax-collector, in whose interest it is to keep the people in arrears. M. de Leval, the good landlord in the above tale, obtains the right to pay the *taille* for his tenants, and by establishing a communal workshop, the profits of which go to the *corvées*, restores happiness and prosperity. If such mutual arrangements could become general, says De Leval, things would right themselves and there would be no need to talk, like the misanthrope, of forming leagues to enforce reform. In Marmontel's work we have a blending of many elements. He is at the same time a novelist of manners, a propagandist, a moralist, a sentimentalist of the type exemplified later in Bernardin de Saint-Pierre. Whatever English atmosphere there is in his novels is due, not so much to the influence of Richardson, but to the Anglo-Saxon ideas which entered France earlier in the century by way of Montesquieu, Prévost and Voltaire.

Mme Elie de Beaumont's *Lettres du marquis de Roselle* were instantly successful both in France and in England, for they were translated into English in 1764, the very year of their appearance in Paris. As the novel was in the form of letters, the critic who noticed it in the current number of the *Monthly Review* referred to it as "an imitation of the epistolary manner of Richardson . . . superior to most of the copies in respect to good sense and that knowledge of the world which constitutes the chief merit of all works of this kind." Yet in reality Mme de Beaumont reminds us very little of Richardson, despite the eulogy of *Clarissa* which she imputes to her Mme Narton. In her genius for psychological analysis she is essentially French. Here Marivaux and Crébillon are her models, whilst the subject of her novel, the mad, romantic infatuation of a young aristocrat for a clever courtesan, is obviously inspired by *Manon Lescaut*. Roselle is another Des Grieux, with his unreasoning passion and his disregard for family and social obligations. Mme de Beaumont, however, has gone outside the cadre of Prévost's novel, by emphasising the possible social consequences of Roselle's infatuation and its repercussions within the hero's intimate circle of relations and

friends. Above all, she has given us in Léonor a
detailed study of the courtesan, actress and adven-
turess who, not content with the usual financial
perquisites, aspires to marriage and social advancement. That a Léonor should constitute a domestic
problem is significant: one cannot imagine the
possibility of such a theme in the novel of the early
part of the century. And if we examine the cause of
this new state of things, we find that it is due to the
upsetting of old moral standards, to the substitution
of sensibility for reason as a guide to conduct. Roselle
is at first passionately in love, but when passion has
exhausted itself in vain onslaughts against the in-
flexible resistance of Léonor, it is transformed into
acute sensibility. Roselle, hoodwinked by the astute
display of mock virtue, is caught up in a wave of
pity for this pure and helpless woman. As his sister's
wise friend, Mme Narton, realises, he is a sick man,
a victim of the malady called Romanticism, which
gathers fresh strength from the well-meaning opposi-
tion of friends. Here already we have the "grand
incompris" of the Romantic period, the victim of
society, the implacable enemy which would rob him
of his love. Interference by his blundering brother-
in-law precipitates events, and Roselle strikes down
his dearest friend, who forces him to read the damning
letters containing evidence of Léonor's perfidy. Mme
de Beaumont was too much of an artist to leave the
story here. Roselle is morally shattered: but he is
still in love with Léonor, and were it not for what
he calls his honour, in reality his amour-propre, he

would go back to his mistress. His cynical and Crébillonesque friend Valville prescribes an affair or two
with society women as a tonic, which gives the author
a chance for a diatribe against the corruption of that
"national menace," *la bonne compagnie*. The novel
becomes now an excuse for what Valville airily refers
to as "la haute morale." Roselle finds consolation in
the soothing atmosphere of the ideal family circle of
the bourgeoise Mme de Ferval. Education is one of
Mme de Beaumont's hobbies, and she now rides it
fairly hard. Like so many eighteenth-century femi-
nists, Mme de Ferval's chief preoccupation is the
transference of the education of the young girl from
the convent to the home, for the secret of character-
training is complete sympathy between mother and
daughter. There must be no intermediary, for this
sacred duty cannot be entrusted to servants or
governesses. "La bonté est la base de tout," says this
excellent woman, and by "bonté" she does not mean
sentimentality, but a carefully directed sensibility
which does not dissipate itself in an objectless way, but
is lavish in its response to really deserving appeals.

Roselle is cured of his melancholy by contact
with this *milieu*, and Léonor's attempt to reinstate
herself finds him well armed. There is nothing idealistic about the fate of this courtesan: she does not,
like Manon, "purify" herself by a picturesque death.
On the contrary, she sinks into abject poverty, is
aided by the marquise de Roselle, and vanishes
decently into a convent—a prosaic, but most probable
ending to an excellent novel.

CHAPTER XI

THE INFLUENCE OF JEAN-JACQUES ROUSSEAU

As a result of a series of delays, some due to bad luck, and others to difficulties with the censorship, Rousseau's eagerly awaited novel, *La Nouvelle Héloïse*, was not exposed for sale in Paris until February 1761. It had been known in London, however, since November of the preceding year, when the *Monthly Review* gave a brief notice to the book, reserving its final judgment for the English translation, which was not completed till early in 1762. The reviewer remarked, in 1760, that Rousseau seemed to have had "the writings of the celebrated Richardson in view," and later, in a more considered summing-up, observed: "Though Mr. Rousseau falls short in many respects of Mr. Richardson, whose manner he has imitated, yet in others he so far excels him as to appear himself an inimitable original. There are many persons who do not scruple to say they admire the character of Eloisa beyond that of Clarissa." When we consider the circumstances—for the English novelist was in the full flush of his fame—this was praise indeed. Comparison with Richardson was inevitable, and imposed itself on all contemporary critics. In more recent times, for critics, like historians, repeat each other, similar parallels have been drawn by French writers, in particular by Joseph Texte, who devotes several pages to an attempt to prove an indebtedness which is, I feel, largely imaginary, since it rests on circumstances necessitated by the employment of the letter form, which Rousseau did indeed borrow from Richardson. Texte's method is to draw up parallel lists of characters which of course offer traits of similarity. For example, Clarissa's father, like Julie's, is harsh; Rousseau's heroine Julie resembles Clarissa in her gravity; Claire, Julie's confidante, is gay like Miss Howe; Julie's letters, like those of Clarissa, are intercepted. He goes on to point out that Julie, like Clarissa, has a devoted friend and similarly has a male confidant, Bomston, who in Rousseau's novel, however, is also a friend of the hero's. He might also have added that Julie, like Clarissa, had a mother! It would have been just as convincing as the other so-called parallels. Admittedly no writer is immune from the influence of his century, not even a highly individual genius like Rousseau, but it is to Jean-Jacques' own experiences, and not to Richardson's novel, that we must look if we would discover the inspiration which prompted him to write the *Nouvelle Héloïse*. I do not believe, with Texte, that Rousseau learned from the Englishman the art of portraying and presenting his characters, nor that his eloquence and sensibility came from this source. A brief analysis of the *Nouvelle Héloïse* will reveal immediate divergences between the two novels which, so to speak, leap to the eye.

Rousseau's object was to write a bourgeois novel

with a salutary moral, an antidote to the typical French novel of high life, which usually ridiculed provincials and made them discontented with their lot. He therefore chose his characters in the ranks of the upper and middle classes. Julie, the heroine, is the daughter of the baron d'Etanges, a Swiss country squire, whilst Saint-Preux, her lover, is a tutor, and the impoverished son of an army officer. The scene of the novel is a small country district at the foot of the Alps, a circumstance which allowed the author free scope for his well-known naturist propaganda. We are introduced to the chief actors at a critical moment in their emotional experience. Saint-Preux, who has long been in love with Julie's virtue and sentimental charm, at last declares himself a victim to her "quick sensibility and unchangeable sweetness." Julie, hitherto the soul of gaiety, becomes melancholy and capricious. Unable to keep silent, she writes a passionate letter to Saint-Preux, in which she admits defeat, upbraids her lover as a "vile seducer," and throws herself on his mercy. Saint-Preux's natural goodness and sympathy and his adoration of her virtue, hold his senses in check for a time. Julie confides in her friend Claire, who trembles for the future. One word to Mme d'Etanges at this stage would, of course, have saved Julie, but she wants "to escape the danger of yielding, but not the honour of struggling." She realises that this is the crisis, that the slightest alteration in her present conduct will open the door to a lifetime of remorse and misery. Saint-Preux's dumb suffering, his obvious self-restraint, the impossibility of marriage, and the contrast in their lot, fill her with a surging and unbounded pity. She kisses him, and thus lets loose a torrent of passionate desire. Her pity is her undoing. Her father has made it plain that she is to marry one of his friends, M. de Wolmar, and Julie, in despair, and not daring to tell her lover that his hope of marriage can never be realised, yields. Her remorse is terrible, yet she is happy so long as her lover is with her.

From this moment her initiative stands out in sharp contrast to the passionate and lyric inactivity of Saint-Preux, who is perfectly content to seize the "crowded hour of glorious life," and willingly surrenders his destiny to Julie, who schemes to arrange future interviews at the house of Claire, and finally introduces her lover into her room at night. The reason advanced by Rousseau for this second lapse is plausible but scarcely convincing. Julie, who looks on herself as Saint-Preux's "sainte épouse," feels that maternity would solve her difficulties, for, if her father saw the tangible results of her guilt, he would either consent to marriage or kill her. It is difficult here, as in other points in this narrative, to follow the author's logic: surely the same result would be achieved by the public confession of her relations with Saint-Preux, which indeed she proposes to make. M. d'Etanges hears of his daughter's familiarity with the low-born tutor, but fortunately does not guess the truth. Saint-Preux has to go away to Paris, and leaves after scenes of unimaginable grief.

Mme d'Etanges, whose foolish negligence was largely responsible for her daughter's downfall, dies. Lord Edward Bomston, a typical *honnête homme* who has had the confidence of the lovers all along, offers to settle them on one of his English estates. Julie's sense of duty to her father makes her reject this proposal, and after obtaining unwilling permission from her anguished lover, she marries M. de Wolmar, another *honnête homme* who is, however, a sceptic in religion. At this point we note a complete change in the character of Julie which cannot be explained by her marriage. It was already improbable that Julie d'Etanges would have allowed her filial respect to deprive her of a Heaven-sent opportunity of marriage with Saint-Preux, but it is still more unlikely that the old Julie, even though she was nicknamed playfully ''Julie la prêcheuse,'' could be transformed into the didactic, argumentative and sententious person we find in Julie de Wolmar.

After years spent in travel, Saint-Preux returns and is invited by Wolmar to live with his wife and himself. To fully appreciate the situation we must know that Julie has not yet confessed all the truth about her relations with Saint-Preux, though Wolmar knows it and, moreover, knew it before he married her. The ex-lover is told candidly that absolute frankness is the tone of the establishment, and Wolmar adopts towards him the attitude of a father speaking to a prodigal son. In order to test Saint-Preux, to whom he proposes entrusting the education of his children, Wolmar leaves him with Julie for a week. A critical scene is enacted amongst the rocks of Meillerie, whither Saint-Preux had gone ten years previously to await Julie's permission to return. Drawn invincibly to this spot, Saint-Preux makes a supreme effort to recapture Julie, but realises that she has changed irrevocably. Returning homeward by moonlight to Clarens, the home of the Wolmars, Saint-Preux is shaken by a last gust of passion, and is tempted to kill her and himself. A gentler sentiment steals over him, and his mad passion vanishes in a paroxysm of weeping.

The days steal past in a sort of Arcadia where everyone is happy because everyone is good, and where Julie, the perfect wife and mother, exposes Rousseau's theories on religion, education and economy. She has passed through the various stages of guilty passion, remorse, confession, renunciation, and is now rehabilitated. Now she has only to die and be canonised. Her son falls into the water, and in rescuing him she catches some mysterious malady which enables her to spend a few days in dying. "You have lived for charity," says the venerable Protestant pastor, "you die a martyr to maternal love." Her one regret is that Wolmar is not yet converted, but that task she delegates, in her last letter, to Saint-Preux. She realises before her death that she has been living in a state of illusion, for she still loves Saint-Preux. "Everything that depends on my will is on the side of duty: if my heart, which does not depend on that, was for you," she tells her lover, "that was my punishment and not my crime.

I have done what I ought to have done. My virtue remains stainless, and I have kept my love without remorse. . . . That virtue which kept us apart on earth will unite us in the eternal abode."

The book naturally aroused a storm of protest from critics like Marmontel, who exclaimed against the immorality of rehabilitating a fallen woman. Others observed that the novel was moral in theory and immoral in practice. Women like the comtesse de Polignac went mad over it, because, as Rousseau shrewdly pointed out, they suspected it was his love story. This fact, said the author coolly, showed that they failed to understand to what degree he could become inflamed by purely imaginary creations. He confessed, however, to "some youthful memories of Mme d'Houdetot." *La Nouvelle Héloïse* is, in fact, a patchwork of personal experiences and impressions. Julie herself is an ideal creation, partly Mme de Warens, Rousseau's first mistress, and partly Mme d'Houdetot, whose affections he shared, *à la* Wolmar, with his friend Saint-Lambert. The extraordinary idea of the triple *ménage* had its counterpart also at Les Charmettes, where Rousseau and a robust, serious manservant, Claude Anet, vied with each other in friendship, despite their common relations with the too tender "maman," as Jean-Jacques used to call Mme de Warens. If we are to understand the spirit of the novel, says Rousseau, we must possess a sixth sense, "le sens moral." Most of us, I fear, fail to appreciate it just for that reason. Notwithstanding our modern novelists with their specious talk of "tolerance on sex questions," which is ill-disguised Rousseauism, there is still a deep-rooted prejudice which leads men to demand chastity in their fiancées, and which firmly shuts the door against the Saint-Preux of real life. One cannot for a moment doubt the sincerity of Rousseau's moral intentions, but society can scarcely adopt his doctrines because of that. And yet we have but to glance at current life and literature to see what a profound influence these doctrines still exercise: for *La Nouvelle Héloïse* is the first Romantic novel, and Romanticism, which is now in its sixth generation, is strongly reflected in twentieth-century civilisation.

Romanticism is essentially the vindication of the right of the individual to develop his ego, notwithstanding the prohibitions created by society. That these prohibitions are the product of reason, tradition or experience is beside the point, because the individual, according to Rousseau, has the prior claim since he is following the dictates of Nature. The voice of Nature or the voice of God, for to the Romantic they are identical, whispers simultaneously to Julie and to Saint-Preux that they are destined for each other—a sophistry in which it is easy to catch echoes of Platonism. In the poetic language of Saint-Preux, "our souls have touched." But, though the woman would be content with purely Platonic relations, the "voice of Nature" reminds Saint-Preux that it is natural for men to have senses. For a time his idealism finds a lyrical outlet in an imaginary harmony with external nature, which

thus becomes an accomplice to his love. In his ecstasy,
physical sensation and idealised love are blended, and
find utterance in magnificent prose poetry. From the
first both the lovers cherish the illusion that they
are chosen souls, and that God favours their union.
A growing irritation at the obstacles opposed by
economic and social exigencies confirms them in
their belief that society is fundamentally corrupt.
They agree that only God can attack the institution
of marriage. The only possible social order, says
Saint-Preux, is that in which rank is regulated by
merit, and in which the union of hearts depends on
mutual choice. His immediate sensual desires satisfied,
he loses himself in contemplation of nature, now
their "nuptial couch," and pleasing visions of a life
of undisturbed happiness amidst valleys, hills and
woods strike a lyrical chord in his poetic soul. Baffled
by Julie's decision to sacrifice their love to filial duty,
he meditates murder and suicide—rather illogically,
one feels, because, as Julie points out, she is but
following the *voix de la nature*. The awkward thing
about this apparently simple method of substituting
sentiment for reason as a guide to conduct is to distinguish which sentiment is most natural, and which
should have the prior claim. It is difficult, too, unless
one is a confirmed Rousseauist, to see eye to eye with
Julie in her sententious reflections on entering church
to be married. She vows inwardly to be worthy of her
sacred trust, and regards her marriage to Wolmar as
"a holy bond" which will purify her soul. An hour's
mystic communion with God and her absent lover

convinces her that she has really changed. "My conscience and my senses were tranquil." She is, however,
strong enough to reject Saint-Preux's Romantic and
adulterous proposals, and to refute his objections to
a confession — objections based on the sophism that
her engagement to Wolmar is not retroactive — a
sophism which by the way is actually accepted by
some American jurists.

Julie carries her Romantic and naturist ideas into
her religious life since, as she thinks, "every false
religion combats nature." Also, in her house the female
servants are kept separate from the men in a gynæ-
ceum because savages, that is, natural men, live in
this fashion. Her life is now a perfectly happy one.
She has lifted a burden from her conscience by con-
fessing to her husband, and, as her adoring Claire
points out, she is guilty only in the eyes of men and
not in the sight of God. Now there is only one thing
left, she reflects, as she gazes at her happy circle, and
that is to die. In true Romantic vein she exclaims:
"I am too happy. Happiness wearies me. My heart does
not know what it lacks. It desires it knows not what!"
Her soul revives in contemplation of God, but she is
inconsistent enough to reject the mystic quietism of
a Fénelon, her last concession to classicism and to
reason. The *Nouvelle Héloïse* represents only a stage
in Rousseau's Romantic evolution, and in order to
understand it we must read it in conjunction with
the *Confessions* and the *Rêveries d'un Promeneur
solitaire*. Still, even considered by itself, the novel
presents new and profoundly suggestive tendencies,

for Rousseau, breaking with the literary convention of centuries, boldly identifies himself with his hero. *La Nouvelle Héloïse* is thus the first subjective novel, and opens the way to a new school of personal literature. He is the direct ancestor of Goethe (*Werther*) and of Chateaubriand (*René*), not to speak of Mme de Staël, Scott, Eliot, Brontë, Flaubert in his early manner, Proust, and scores of others who have been influenced by his analytic, subjective method, though they have not always adopted his doctrines.

Yet possibly his greatest service to literature was the stimulus he gave to poetry, in particular to lyric poetry, a genre which had been neglected in France since the Renaissance. In the eighteenth century, naturally enough, the cult of reason was unfavourable to the florescence of lyricism, and sensibility, as we have observed, assumed an objective form, finding an outlet in humanitarian and philanthropic aspirations. By vindicating the right of the individual to afford free play to the passion of love, both in language and in fact, Rousseau heralded that magnificent tempest of lyricism which a hundred years ago broke loose upon a startled Europe. His confusion of love with religious mysticism, his high conception of the function of the poet-lover, and his discovery of external nature as a fitting cadre to passionate love, were elements woven by Lamartine, Hugo, De Musset and De Vigny into the glistering fabric of their poetry. Indeed, many of the letters of the *Nouvelle Héloïse* are unrhymed lyric poems. "Ce sont des hymnes," as Rousseau rightly said in his preface. This annexation of lyricism by the novel marks an important epoch, though it will be remembered that the novel was originally a species of poem. It is significant in this connection to recollect Jean-Jacques' passionate admiration for the *Astrée*, that highly *romanesque* and idealistic, though not Romantic, novel written early in the seventeenth century by Honoré d'Urfé. It was through a rosy veil of Astrean and Biblical memories, too, that he saw the familiar occupations of the country in the *Nouvelle Héloïse*. "It is pleasant to consider the work of the countryside . . . it recalls to the mind agreeable visions, and to the heart the charms of the age of gold." The famous description of the grape harvest at Clarens is an excellent illustration of Rousseau's pastoral manner. In transmuting observed facts, he suppresses those which might detract from the harmony of the completed picture and thus destroy the illusion of a benevolent, fruitful Nature rewarding the toil of her simple children. He is the founder of the novel of rustic manners, and of the regionalist novel, for it is a curious fact that, with the exception of Scarron's *Roman comique*, which is a caricature, no previous novel, except the *Voyage de Mantes*, had described country life and ways. We know that the great mass of aristocratic society spent its summers in rustic surroundings, yet one misses in the French novel of the seventeenth and eighteenth centuries that open-air atmosphere which this Swiss brought from his mountains and wooded valleys. But, for Rousseau the Romantic, Nature is more than a beautiful spectacle: her infinite variety provides a series of settings matching in colour the moods of her devotees. Saint-Preux, like the heroes of Prévost and Tencin, takes his passion and melancholy to the grandeur and awful solitude of rugged Meillerie. The familiar scenes revive his passion, and when he realises that his appeals awaken no response, he leaves Meillerie for ever, "as if," he says, "I were leaving Julie herself."

I have indicated innovations which, it is easy to see, were destined to lend new and tremendous vitality to the novel—lyricism, Romanticism and appreciation of the beauty of nature. Let us see now how far Rousseau carries on the traditions of the French novel. He tells us in his *Confessions* that all his life he was haunted by the misfortune of Prévost's Cleveland. Yet he was the least literary of French novelists, and imitated very little. An allusion in the *Confessions* suggests that he had *La Princesse de Clèves* in mind when he conceived the confession scene in *La Nouvelle Héloïse*. Of Richardson he speaks but seldom, and always in terms of great admiration. There is no reason to assume, like Texte, that Rousseau was jealous of the Englishman just because, in commenting on the large number of characters in the latter's works, he pointed out that this was not a merit, but a defect which Richardson had in common with the most insipid novelists, who usually supplement the sterility of their genius in this way. This statement of fact reveals nothing, save that Rousseau preferred the French to the English tradition. I do not think that Rousseau had ever any doubt as to the superiority of his novel over *Clarissa*. He notes complacently a point barely commented upon by the public, namely the simplicity of his subject, and the sustaining of the interest through six volumes "sans épisode, sans aventure romanesque," a circumstance which, he thinks, will always make the *Nouvelle Héloïse* a unique work. In his naïve vanity he fails to see that his numerous digressions, though more bearable in the epistolary form than in any other, suspend the action of the novel. His reader will also probably disagree with him as to the credibility of some of the episodes which form the armature of the narrative. Like the propagandist novelists of his time, Jean-Jacques does not scruple to make his book a vehicle for his views on society, philosophy, religion and political economy. It will be noted that most of this material is in that part of the novel which deals with the life of Julie married. The reason can be guessed. The main interest of the novel proper disappears with her decision to marry Wolmar: for the virtuous married woman offers little scope for the imagination of the novelist. To revive interest in Julie, Rousseau is driven to the improbable expedient of the triple *ménage*, which indeed holds out possibilities of a relapse and a consequent restatement of the original problem. But this cannot be done without upsetting the whole plan of the novel, which is designed to show the happy result of true repentance. Julie therefore ceases to have any real significance, and becomes a mouthpiece for Rousseau's moral and social doctrines, which indeed have interest, but an interest which derives not from the story, but from the personality of Jean-Jacques.

In the last analysis, then, *La Nouvelle Héloïse* is Romantic in effect, though not in intention. Its moral, to which Marmontel and others took grave exception, is simply an elaboration of the Christian doctrine of the efficacy of true repentance. Our generation, which has the advantage of perspective, realises that Rousseau, in writing his novel, was torn between two contradictory desires: to give rein, on the one hand, to his individual passions in defiance of the dictates of reason and of society, and, on the other, to respect the sanctity of the social order as manifested in the institutions of marriage and of the family. As M. Daniel Mornet, his gifted editor, has pointed out, the key to the apparent enigma is to be found in Rousseau's infatuation for Mme d'Houdetot, which, like Saint-Preux, he eventually renounced to follow the dictates of conscience. We must also take into account the state of contemporary opinion, which, though surcharged with sensibility, was not yet prepared to sacrifice society to the ego. The seeds of Romanticism, however, were sown, though two generations were to elapse before they came to maturity. Meanwhile novelists devoted themselves to the cult of sensibility as a source of delicious suffering, not entirely free from a certain refined sensuality. The old renunciation *motif* of the sentimental novels of the late seventeenth century found new expression in the passionate and poetic language of the *Nouvelle*

Héloïse. In the average novel conscience acquires her rights, though frequently at the expense of probability, and the moral ending is too often tagged on as a concession to convention and as a belated antidote to an orgy of emotional self-flagellation.

The novel becomes more romanesque than ever in response to the demand for stronger emotions, and, significantly enough, a new edition of Tencin's *Malheurs de l'Amour* appears in 1766. It is possible to discern in the novel from Rousseau to the Revolution echoes of every writer of note from Lafayette to Jean-Jacques. English influence, particularly that of Richardson, is less evident, though a casual glance at titles might lead the superficial observer to imagine the contrary. Mme le Prince de Beaumont, so often confused with the authoress of *Les Lettres de Roselle*, Mme Elie de Beaumont, is a good example of this so-called English influence. Her *Nouvelle Clarisse* (1767) has nothing Richardsonian save its title: if anything, it is an imitation of the pastoral, golden age idea exploited by Rousseau and others. One would never guess, were it not for D'Hémery's *Notes de Police sur les Écrivains français*, that Mme de Beaumont spent most of her life in London. There is of course no doubt that translations of English novels were eagerly read along with many others that purported to be so, just as the English public devoured translations of French novels. There was, in fact, a sentimental *entente*. Novelists, both English and French, agreed in regarding the novel as a means of inculcating the high moral doctrines of humanity,

friendship and virtue. As Marmontel put it: "In our
fiction, it is not enough to imitate nature: we must
purify her." It would be wrong, however, to assume,
as many have done, that the English conception of
the art of the novelist, in particular that of Richardson, fundamentally influenced French writers. Mutual
admiration does not necessarily lead to imitation.
The Anglomania of the second half of the eighteenth
century was, as La Dixmérie says, more a question
of fashion than of inherent taste in so far as the novel
was concerned. It did not give rise to new tendencies
in the French novel, though it certainly did much to
consolidate the moral and sentimental type of fiction.
The gloomy, melancholy trend which in the age of
Louis XVI. was considered so typically English, the
genre triste, was, says Grimm in 1774, supposed by
the English to be due to French influence, and indeed we have seen its origins in the novels of Prévost. Anglo-French interaction in the novel of the
eighteenth century existed: that much is clear. French
novelists borrowed an occasional situation from
Richardson and, in deference to the *étrangeromanie*
of the day, inserted references to fashionable English
novelists in their fictions, to which they tried to lend
an English air by the use of Anglo-Saxon proper
and geographical names. One can see evidence of this
sort of literary cosmopolitanism in the extraordinary
attempts of our contemporary English novelists to
lend what they confidently believe to be a Gallic
atmosphere to their works. But influence of this sort
does not touch the essential genius of a race, and

that is why, as we shall see, the French novel of the
late eighteenth century remained quite French, not
only in the type of life it reflected, but in its approach
to that type of life.

The moral purpose of *Les Sacrifices de l'Amour*
(1771), we are told by its author, Dorat, is to prove,
on the one hand, that a woman in love can fulfil all
the duties which oppose her passion, and be all the
more interesting on that account; on the other, to
show that there is no sacrifice which such a woman
cannot obtain from the most passionate lover, if he
is worthy of her love. It is not difficult, of course, to
catch here an echo of the Julie of the Mme d'Houdetot
phase in this ideal and poetic conception of love. It
is the old tale of frustrated love, of a woman forced
into marriage with a jealous old tyrant by a harsh,
materialistic parent. What is refreshing is the echo of
the lyric note of the *Nouvelle Héloïse*, in the passionate
letters of the chevalier de Versenai to the heroine
Mme de Senanges. Here, as with Rousseau, the woman
gives free utterance to her passion, throwing herself
on the mercy of her lover. For Dorat, who is a greater
poet than novelist, nature is an essential part of
love, and all his emotional passages are enacted in
surroundings which harmonise with the sentiments
expressed. "Nous aurons le plus beau clair de lune
du monde," cries the lover, "sa lumière est faite pour
l'amour." The critical scene in the novel, which
takes place in the garden on a summer night, with
the lover keeping ecstatic vigil over his unconscious,
sleeping mistress, is as lyrical as a passage from

Rostand. Mme de Senanges, unable to trust herself, seeks refuge from her passion in the solitude of the mountains, but the majestic, brooding calm brings no relief, for "these haunts of melancholy breed love in tender hearts by the very sadness which they inspire."

The correspondence of the lovers is a delirious *cri de cœur*. "Rendons-nous à la nature" is the burthen of the chevalier's letters, while Mme de Senanges rages against society: "O frightful vice of our legislation! Everywhere fetters, prejudices and misfortune! Everywhere the heart in contradiction with the law! Tyranny ever sacred whatever form it takes, and nature prostituted to the vilest conventions of man!" Yet she immolates herself to duty, which she interprets as the literal observance of her marriage vows. "The evil lies in yielding, not in feeling," she tells her lover, and she does not yield, for luckily death removes the wicked husband and the lovers are united—a concession to morality at the expense of probability, which prompted the sardonic Grimm to suggest as an amendment to the original title: "Les sacrifices du bon sens de l'auteur à la pauvreté de son imagination."

One current of the sentimental novel continued to move farther and farther from the reality of life, towards the realms of idealism. It is significant that the author of the popular *Les Egarements de l'Amour* (1776) was, like Dorat, poet as well as novelist, as was also Léonard, who, in his *Lettres de deux Amants* (1783), blended the sombre manner of a D'Arnaud with the idyllism of Gessner, whose poetry vied with Young's *Night Thoughts* in popularity. The favourite literature of France on the eve of revolution consisted largely of such Utopian, idyllic novels as are described by L. S. Mercier, the "dramomane," in the following passage taken from his *Bonnet de Nuit* (1784):

> There is another sort of novel dear to the philosopher. It is that which presents an ideal plan of public and national felicity—a consoling dream which dimly reveals that in the future men will combine the light of their reason and the courage of their soul to counterbalance the evils of nature and the faults of their ancestors. The friend of mankind breathes again when he peruses these works, which, though fantastic, are yet sweet to read. He fears only the moment when his dream will disappear.

Such an anodyne was offered by Bernardin de Saint-Pierre in his *Paul et Virginie* (1787), which earned for its author a fame that spread beyond the confines of France far over Europe. One could invert Dr. Johnson's saying regarding *Pamela* in speaking of *Paul et Virginie*, for the reader might as well hang himself as read it for its morality, which is that of a hundred other novels of the period. Here it is the tale that counts. A confirmed Utopian, Saint-Pierre was a fervent admirer of Jean-Jacques Rousseau, with whom he quarrelled on every possible occasion, as indeed he did with everyone he ever knew. He conceived his *Paul et Virginie*, he tells us, in a respite from his long, pseudo-scientific treatise called *Etudes sur la Nature* in which, calmly ignoring the discoveries of scientists like Newton, he interpreted nature as

the handiwork of a benevolent Creator who made
fleas brown so that they might be easily detected
against the white skin of their victims, and ribbed
the melon as an indication that this "social fruit"
was intended to be eaten *en famille*! But this eccentric
had the precious gift of acute observation and the
artist's eye for colour and harmony. His search for
a country in which to establish an Arcadian republic
drove him from Europe to Mauritius, then called
Île de France, and so it was that he conceived as a
setting for his idyllic story of the life and love of
Paul and Virginie a tropical, sea-girt land of waving
palms and blossoming lemon-trees.

Mme de la Tour, the daughter of a noble family,
has to leave France with her low-born husband, to
escape the persecution of her parents. The young
couple arrive at Mauritius, where a child, Virginie,
is born. De la Tour, on a trading expedition to Mada-
gascar, dies of fever, leaving his wife alone, save for
a faithful negress. But there is another fugitive from
the evils of society, Marguerite, a woman of Breton
peasant stock, seduced and basely deserted by a
nobleman. These tender souls are drawn together by
the common bonds of misfortune and sensibility, and
in Paul, Marguerite's little son, Virginie finds a companion, for the parents agree that the children will
grow up to enjoy the pleasures of happiness and
equality far from the cruel prejudices of Europe.
Nature is their only teacher, and they are kept in
blissful ignorance of the terrors of the Christian
religion.

So their childhood glides past, says Saint-Pierre, "like a lovely dawn heralding a still more lovely day." To while away the long summer evenings the children act scenes from the Bible in the forest glades, where "the setting sun's rays, broken by the tree-trunks, converge in the shadows of the forest in long sheaves of light." The novel is drenched with colour. "The foliage of the trees, lit from beneath by saffron rays, shone with the fires of topaz and emerald. Their mossy brown trunks seemed changed into columns of antique bronze: and the birds, already wrapped in silence under the sombre foliage, surprised to see a second dawn, saluted the orb of day with a thousand songs." So one could go on quoting, for Saint-Pierre is rich in such descriptions. An idealist in questions of morality, he is a realist in the precision with which he reproduces his memory-pictures of exotic nature. Nightfall in the forest, a tropical rainstorm, the riot of colour on a hillside, the witchery and perfume of an Eastern night, leap into vivid reality at his command. He is a poet and a great artist. With him exoticism enters the French novel. The beauty and mystery of strange and distant climes glimpsed in *Robinson Crusoe*—even then a household book in France—and in the voyagers' tales of Tavernier, Chardin and Bernier, now found complete artistic expression. *Paul et Virginie* gave the French of the time of Louis XVI. the picture of exotic nature which they wanted, a Mauritius of gentle, sentimental savages and brutal whites, a smiling, fruitful Eden, with no serpent and only occasional hurricanes, which, by their spectacular magnificence, amply compensated for the material damage they might cause.

Evil, then, can only come from civilisation, and its representatives here are the missionary of the Church and the governor of the State. At the request of a great-aunt in France, Virginie is forced to go to Paris, to become an heiress. Here Saint-Pierre attains a high level of poetry and tragedy. Virginie, now on the brink of womanhood, is stirred with vague but poignant longings, and in a superb nocturne the author describes the dawn of passion in a virginal soul. Economic difficulties stand in the way of marriage, for the two mothers are growing old. The governor uses his authority to oblige her to leave, and the missionary tells her that it is the will of God. Paul, who now knows the secret of his birth, suffers all the misery which accompanies the sentiment of social inferiority in a youthful mind. His mad grief persuades Mme de la Tour to relinquish the scheme, but the governor forces her hand, and Virginie is hurried off. Time passes, and Virginie, who is unhappy in Paris, finally resolves to set sail for Mauritius, so that in due course her ship is sighted outside the harbour of the island.

But at the eleventh hour happiness eludes the lovers. The *Saint Géran* is to land in the morning, but during the night a hurricane drives her ashore. Within sight of the islanders the great vessel is slowly ground against the rocks. The crew throw themselves into the water, and Paul makes frantic efforts to

reach Virginie, who is still on the deck of the founder-
ing ship. The last sailor to leave tries to rescue her,
but she refuses to disrobe, her only chance of reaching
safety. Rather than do this she drowns, preferring
death to what she considers immodesty. Paul dies
of grief, and is soon followed by his mother and Mme
de la Tour. The cabins moulder away: the beasts
and birds vanish, and the cry of the hawk alone
breaks the silence that broods over the home of these
immortal lovers. There are some books which it is
almost a sacrilege to criticise. There are not many,
but *Paul et Virginie* is one of them. Its defects are
obvious to the most untutored eye: it is easy to laugh
at its old-world and naïve morality. Yet it has
charmed generations of different races, because it
has the two great qualities of all classics: sympathy
and sincerity.

Some names will always live in the history of
literature, not because they are associated with works
of lasting value, but because they conjure the image
of a sweet and gentle personality. The name of Florian,
"le gentil Florianet," as Voltaire called him, evokes
the close of an era which, to the last, remained in-
curably sentimental and tragically optimistic. In all
Florian's work, for he was a playwright and fabulist
as well as a novelist, the outstanding quality is
sweetness, tinged with an autumnal and elegiac note.
Florian lived in an illusory past, a world of romance,
chivalry and pastoral delights. Of his contemporaries
only Gessner really attracted him. "If I were a village
priest," he said earnestly, "I would read at my

services the works of Gessner, and I am quite sure
that all the peasants would become honest men, and
all the women of my parish chaste." It was the poetry
of Gessner and Thomson that inspired Florian to
write his pastoral novel *Estelle et Nemorin* (1787), in
the preface to which he exposes his theories on this
type of fiction. The pastoral novel as conceived by
Florian is partly in prose and partly in verse, a story
of the joy and sorrow of true love, for love must
always be sacrificed to duty, to preserve that "degree
of utility" which is the aim of every good writer.
In *Estelle et Nemorin* Florian satisfied his longing to
re-live the happy days of his childhood, and so his
shepherds and shepherdesses spend their golden
days on the banks of the Gardon, in Florian's native
Beaurivage. "It is so sweet," he confesses, "to speak of
our native land and to remember the places where we
spent our early years. Their very names have a secret
charm for our soul." There are no wicked shepherds
in Florian's Arcadia, and even when he describes the
invasion of this perfect country by the Spaniards,
he evokes a picture of gentle, high-souled warriors
who kill each other with the greatest reluctance and
in the most courteous way imaginable. Poor Florian's
Utopia was in the past, not in the future. With his
Galatée (1783) and his *Estelle* the sentimental and
moral novel reverts to its original type, and we must
go back farther even than the *Astrée* to find a parallel,
back to Longus' *Daphnis et Chloé*, since Florian's
characters have none of the subtlety and precious
gallantry of D'Urfé's Céladon and Astrée.

This retrogression is quite natural, and was inevitable. The French novelist of the latter half of the eighteenth century, in attempting to make the novel a vehicle for propaganda, diverted it from its true function, which is not to portray life as it ought to be, but to present a probable image of life as it is. I do not mean to imply that there are not good novels which contain a measure of idealism, of morality, and of instruction. That would be absurd and untrue. It is entirely a question of proportion. The literature of eighteenth-century France is strewn with well-meaning attempts at novels which are really political treatises, religious tracts, Utopian schemes of educational reform, pseudo-histories, and voyages and prose poems. In every case their author missed the mark because he subordinated the novel proper to the object he had in view, and for which the novel was a mere excuse. And yet, in this respect, the eighteenth-century novelist enjoyed a latitude which has never since been accorded to writers of fiction, for his public was in a quite peculiar psychological state. As we turn over the pages of these sentimental and didactic productions, with their pretty-pretty engravings by Marillier and Eisen, a growing feeling of wonder and pity steals over us. For after all, this was the favourite literature of a people on the verge of cataclysmal changes, a nation which took refuge from the ugliness of reality in a world of romance and sentimentality. Thousands found their nepenthe in fiction of this kind. A strange state of mind, it is true, yet one which our generation is peculiarly able to understand and to condone, for are we not passing through a somewhat similar phase in our instinctive distaste for literature which reminds us even remotely of the realities of our recent war madness?

CHAPTER XII

IF we now view in retrospect those tendencies which we have been tracing in the novel from the Renaissance to the eve of the Revolution, we may find confirmation of a statement advanced at the outset of this study. I said that the history of the development of the French novel was a narrative of the vicissitudes of idealism and realism, the two primary sources of inspiration in all literature. On the whole, the balance between these two tendencies has been fairly maintained, though the Utopianism and sentimentality of the late eighteenth-century novelists came near to annihilating the novel as a separate genre, by depriving it of its distinctive characteristic, its fidelity to life, of which it is, or ought to be, a probable reflection. But we must not ignore a compensating movement towards reality which has been in progress during the whole of this period, and which we observed in the psychological studies offered by Mme de Lafayette, Marivaux, Prévost, Crébillon, Riccoboni and others. In their analysis of the motives which give rise to passion and sentiment, in their portrayal of the habits of mind which constitute character, such writers were realists in the highest sense of the term. But realism has acquired a very special connotation in literature, ever since its association with the works of the nineteenth-century school of so-called realistic novelists: Champfleury, Balzac, Flaubert, Zola, the brothers Goncourt and Maupassant. These writers, to a greater or lesser degree, aimed at the objective reproduction of un-idealised life. As realists they were concerned mostly with the *mœurs* of the lowest classes of society, the people and the *petite bourgeoisie.* We shall see that this conception of reality, which we may call low realism, had its origins in the eighteenth century, though hitherto it has been usual to explain it as a reaction against the Romanticism of the early nineteenth century.

In Laclos' *Liaisons dangereuses* (1782), though we discover a painfully real attitude towards life, the author is not at all concerned with the manners and morals of the lower classes. All his characters belong to the aristocracy, and here of course Laclos is adhering to the traditions observed by Duclos and Crébillon *fils,* whom he most closely resembles. We may be excused from entering into details regarding the situations exposed in this novel, which is a cold and cynical account of the carefully planned and deliberately executed seduction of a young girl, and of a married woman of high principles and delicate scruples. There is a Balzacian quality in Laclos' villains, the infamous marquise de Merteuil and her tool, the vicomte de Valmont, who commit crime for the sheer love of doing evil. "Conquérir est notre

destin," writes Valmont, who is actuated by a demonic
amour-propre in his designs against Mme de Tourvel,
the virtuous wife of a *président à mortier*, or, as we
should say, High Court Judge. The motive alleged
for the action of Mme de Merteuil is primarily revenge,
since her victim, Cécile, is about to marry a former
lover of the marquise. By keeping the two plots
almost separate, Laclos throws into sharp relief certain fundamental differences between the characters
of the two conspirators. The growing intimacy of
Valmont and Mme de Tourvel irritates the marquise,
for whom the corruption of Cécile is the main consideration. With the clairvoyance of the jealous
woman, she realises that Valmont is falling in love,
and trembles for the success of her diabolical plans.
Valmont's procrastination infuriates her, because it
seems so unnecessary to her depraved mind. A sen-
sualist herself, she is utterly incapable of conceiving
virtue in one of her own sex. "Love," according to
her simplist code, "is like medicine, merely an aid to
nature." She therefore pours contempt on Valmont's
tactics, for in her eyes Mme de Tourvel is merely
exercising a feminine privilege so as to be able to
succumb decently, and according to the conventions.
Valmont, on the other hand, is not really interested
in the ingenuous Cécile, not because of any moral
scruples, but because she is easy game. In Mme de
Tourvel, however, he knows that he is attacking a
woman fortified by inherited moral prejudices and
religious beliefs. Her seduction becomes, then, an
intellectual problem demanding long preparation and

consummate acting. "I will dare to ravish her from the very God whom she adores," he cries in a moment of exaltation, and with refined cynicism he feigns conversion, and enlists the innocent aid of Mme de Tourvel's confessor so as to obtain an interview with her.

Laclos' central figures are of course exaggerated beyond the limits permissible even in the portrayal of a type. Valmont, like Richardson's Lovelace, is an example of inverted idealism, the magnification of vice which one meets with, for example, in Balzac's Vautrin. Yet the novel illustrates a very real truth which is implied in the title and further expressed by the author as follows: "Any woman who consents to admit to her intimacy a man of loose morals ends by becoming his victim." *Les Liaisons dangereuses* is therefore really a reply to the *Nouvelle Héloïse*, with its specious, romanesque illusion of a seducer brought back to the path of virtue by the love of a good woman. Even Richardson, whose Clarissa, like Mme de Tourvel, dies of remorse and grief, was sentimental enough to end his novel with the reform of Lovelace. Laclos makes no such concessions. Which is the more probable? I do not think that Laclos took Richardson as his model, though he had certainly read *Clarissa*, and Valmont refers scornfully to the drugging episode in the English novel as a crude proceeding quite foreign to his methods. By a refinement of vice he contemplates a voluntary capitulation of his victim, whose eventual fall becomes thus much more probable, since it is not due to external happenings, but arises logically from the exaggerated sensibility of the heroine, which leads her first to pity, then to love Valmont. It is worth noting, too, as a further instance of Laclos' realistic conception of life, that Mme de Tourvel has no regrets immediately after her lapse. She is perfectly content because she has made her idol happy, and it is only when she realises that he has never loved her that she gives way to remorse and grief. It is unfortunate that Laclos did not manage to shake off the Crébillonesque obsession for erotic and scabrous description which has done so much to hide the really artistic qualities of this novel, and has led so many editors to confuse it with those other, but inferior, productions of the eighteenth century which periodically appear in the form of atrociously translated "rare and curious French novels."

.   .   .   .   .

Historians of French society of the old régime have comparatively little to tell us about the life of the people, which is imperfectly reflected in the literature of the time. One of the great achievements of the nineteenth century was to rectify this anomaly in founding what Hugo called *une littérature démocratique*. When the lower classes appear in the novel of the seventeenth century, as for instance in the works of Scarron and Furetière, they are caricatured and satirised beyond probability. Lesage is guilty of the same fault, and his valets and chambermaids are the conventional, witty and unscrupulous characters whose lineage may be traced back to classic comedy. Marivaux, as we know, incurred considerable odium by daring to present a true portrait of the people, and this aspect of his work was not imitated by the best novelists. Prévost, it will be remembered, had to "chastise" the realistic language of *Pamela*, and Desfontaines in 1742, criticising the translation, praised the English novelist for sparing his public "the disgusting jargon of a low servant or of a man of the dregs of the people. If a servant speaks, it is simply and reasonably, for common sense belongs to all classes, and pleases in the mouth of any character provided it is not degraded by thoughts which smack too much of the lower orders, and which a gentleman does not care to hear." Desfontaines' translation of *Joseph Andrews* (1743) was not a success, and its author was puzzled at the apparent inconsistency of "certain persons of high rank" who were offended by its realism, though they enjoyed the realistic descriptions and the "Flemish pictures" of *Gil Blas*. But the attitude of the public was not illogical. *Joseph Andrews* was a parody of *Pamela*, which had been translated and well received the previous year, so that the moment was hardly propitious. Again, the French reader had long been accustomed to the Gallic wit of *Gil Blas*, with its traditional, picaresque setting. They could not be expected, however, to appreciate the typical humour of Fielding, who has never caught hold of the French imagination. Mme Riccoboni's translation of *Amelia*, for example, was a complete failure, and in the whole century only a few superior minds like Grimm and La Harpe were able to appreciate the genius of Fielding. For the same reason Smollett, as a novelist, did not appeal to the French eighteenth-century public, though as an historian he had more success. The sentimental sly *double-entendre* of Sterne, however, got him many readers in France, where his manner was imitated in particular by Gorgy in his *Nouveau Voyage sentimental*.

At the beginning of the eighteenth century, realism in the novel was chiefly a reaction against the idealised conception of love expressed by writers in the *Clélie* tradition. Mme de Meheust's *Histoire d'Emilie* (1732) is a typical example of this category. Here the sophistication of a precocious *pensionnaire* is cynically opposed to the quixotic and chivalrous love-making of a romanesque hero, whose dalliance infuriates the impatient Emilie. There are several realistic novels of picaresque adventure which continue the seventeenth-century tradition in their cruel satire of the lower classes, but an occasional obscure novelist is found who describes the life of the *peuple* largely from an objective standpoint, or at least with a minimum of satire. Such a writer was the anonymous author of the *Histoire de Gogo* (1739), who gives a realistic account of the adventures of a servant-girl in the underworld of Paris, and with great fidelity reproduces the language and the manners of a class not often met with in the literature of the period outside the annals of the Hôpital prison. From the literary standpoint, of course, such works are worse than mediocre. They have, however, historical significance, since they indicate the existence of an uninterrupted undercurrent of realism, and explain to some extent the sudden florescence of this type of novel in the nineteenth century. There was, all through the eighteenth century, a small but persistent demand for realistic fiction.

About 1745 the whim of a group of fashionables, led by Maurepas and the comte de Caylus, gave rise to a special type of realistic *nouvelle*. Caylus, who used to frequent the Halles, or Billingsgate, of Paris, has left us in his *Lettres de la Grenouillère*, and in his *Fêtes roulantes*, written about 1747, illuminating and sympathetic, though somewhat Rabelaisian sketches of the Paris plebs. His *Histoire de M. Guillaume* is equally interesting, and unfolds a picture of popular manners as seen by a Parisian cab-driver. Others, like Vadé the poet, cultivated this field, but none approach Caylus in fidelity of portraiture. Caylus is in a sense the literary ancestor of Courteline: he has the same irresistible sense of humour, and the same sympathetic qualities.

The eighteenth century can show several novels founded on fact, "documented," as the Goncourts used to say, in their pseudo-scientific jargon, and we know that the seventeenth-century *nouvelle* was frequently based on some contemporary event. De Mouhy and D'Arnaud also romanced current scandals, though the censorship discouraged the practice. Such writers confined themselves to polite society as a rule, but Guer, in his *Pinolet* (1755), conceived the idea of making a novel out of the life-story of a well-known Paris beggar. Guer is a poor stylist, but displays a remarkable knowledge of peasant life and psychology. *Pinolet* is interesting as an indictment of the sordid avarice and brutality of the peasant class, and because of the author's close attention to detail. Guer's realism has echoes of the grossness of the picaresque novel, but the prevailing note is one of sombre disillusionment, which reminds one forcibly of Maupassant's pessimism. Descriptions of peasant life are rare in the French novel of this period. One catches glimpses in De Mouhy's *Paysanne parvenue* of village manners. His peasants really smack of the soil and speak its language. He reveals the peasant's smouldering animosity against the hated tax-farmer, and his jealous suspicion of the "fine gentlemen," whose grand manners turn the heads of the country girls. Coustellier's *Lettres de Montmartre* (1750), written entirely in peasant dialect, is a satire on Marivaux's *Paysan parvenu*, and also on the habits of the *maltôtier*, or tax-collector. Underlying the realistic account of the seamy side of Parisian life is a warning not to leave the country for the city, a theme which we find repeatedly in the later novels of the time.

The growth of sentimentality encouraged the development of low realism. By dwelling on the squalor of the surroundings to which the unfortunate and virtuous heroine was reduced, the pathos of her situation was correspondingly accentuated. Satire disappeared as an adjunct to realism, and soon drunkenness and other social vices ceased to be regarded by novelists as food for merriment. Yet prejudice dies hard, and it was not till late in the century that Rétif de la Bretonne, the son of a Burgundy peasant-farmer, tore away the veil which concealed the life of the lower classes from the reading public.

There is probably nothing which we do not know about the life of this amazing character: if there is, it is because his memory failed him, for in his *Monsieur Nicholas ou le cœur humain dévoilé*, we have the most complete confession ever penned. His novels, too, are composed almost entirely of his personal experiences and those of his friends. Rétif's style is emphatic: he is verbose and didactic; his sentimentality is at times grotesque, but his work holds our attention by its absolute sincerity. A great part of it belongs to the province of psychiatry rather than to that of literary criticism, and this is unfortunate, since it has blinded critics to the originality of this strange man, whose mania for confession was such that he did not hesitate to confide his most intimate thoughts. His first successful work, *Le Paysan perverti* (1775), bears the significant subtitle, *Les Dangers de la Ville*, and in the gradual degeneration of Edmond and his sister Ursule, Rétif has painted a terrible picture of the corrupting effect of city life on the morals of two characters who are weak, but not fundamentally vicious. Edmond is a portrait of the author, and in the downfall of Ursule he has committed the unpardonable error in taste of de-

scribing the experiences of his sister, Marie-Genofève.
The most interesting figure in the novel is, however,
Gaudet d'Arras, the ex-priest, social renegade and
apostle of corruption, who bears a striking resemblance to Balzac's gigantic creation, Carlos Herrera.
Gaudet is an atheist who recognises in nature no
moral power superior to man. He is a Romantic in
his vindication of man's right to suffer no obstacle
to the free exercise of his natural passions. Gaudet
is drawn from real life, and his evil doctrines con-
siderably influenced Rétif at one stage in his career:
the Gaudet of the *Paysan perverti*, however, is mag-
nified to gigantic proportions, which make of him a
striking type of Romantic perversion. He is, in short,
the predecessor of those epic figures we meet in the
novels of Hugo, Balzac and Zola, and which pass
outside the confines of reality into the realm of
inverted idealism.

Like many egomaniacs, Rétif visualised himself as
a prophet and reformer, and in his *Idées singulières*
we find a series of elaborate schemes aiming at the
complete reversal of all existing institutions, and the
re-establishment of society on a communistic basis,
which may well have suggested to Fourier his celebrated system of *phalanstères*. However, the chief
interest of his work lies in its realistic and detailed
picture of the manners of the people, both urban
and rural. From this point of view, all his novels are
documents in spite of their moral and didactic pretensions, and they offer to the historian valuable information about the social and economic life of the

masses on the eve of the Revolution. The *Contemporaines*, for example, form a series of short stories in which Rétif conceived the Balzacian idea of exposing a gallery of social types drawn from some two hundred trades and professions. He intended to indicate the abuses which are associated with certain callings, but does not always identify his heroines in this way, owing to his predilection for sentimental situations. It is not lack of knowledge of life which hampers Rétif, for his experiences were varied and interesting. We have seen, too, that his mind was capable of imagining vast schemes. But his extraordinary egotism deprived him of that faculty of objective observation which characterises the great realists. It is true, of course, that excellent novels have been written by subjective writers. *René*, *Werther* and *Adolphe* are confessions, but they reflect the doubts and strivings of noble minds grappling with the inscrutable mystery of human existence. A personal novel is great only if its author's experience of life has universal import. But Rétif's life, though crowded with interesting adventures, attracts us only because of the *milieu* in which the adventures were enacted. The experiences themselves were for the most part vulgar amours, the mere frequency of which removes them outside the sphere of passion. His erotic promiscuities teach us little because of the exceptional character of Rétif, who was a man of abnormal appetites. A novel consisting of abnormal incidents, however true we may know they are, must always seem an improbable and therefore artistically defective novel. The art of the novelist lies in his ability to present, not what *has* happened in life, but what in the reader's opinion might probably have happened. We say that truth is stranger than fiction: what we mean is that truth is frequently so strange that it makes bad fiction.

Yet in the evolution of the French novel the work of Rétif has an important place, because it represents the link between the low realism of the sentimental school and the objective realism of the nineteenth century. It is significant that Rétif admits having been inspired to begin his *Paysan* by the reading of a fragment of *Pamela*. There is also much in the nickname given him by his century: "the Rousseau of the gutter." He reflects the sentimental, didactic morality of his age: by his subjectivism, he is a pre-Romantic: but he is a realist, because his life was spent amongst the people, and because the personal emotions which he describes were usually of the most sordid kind. He is, in fact, an excellent illustration of the truth of M. Doumic's dictum, quoted at the beginning of this study, that almost anyone can write a novel provided he cares to make the public the confidant of his intimate life.

It is largely through coincidence that the Revolution marks the close of one era in the development of the novel and ushers in the dawn of another. In order to explain the general mediocrity of French literature during the Revolutionary period, critics ordinarily point to the disappearance of the *salons*, the emigration of the nobility, and the censorship, all of which would be excellent reasons if they explained the mediocrity of literature in the years immediately preceding 1789. It is dangerous, I feel, to seek the causes of literary evolution only in political history, and if we examine these statements in their relation to one type of literature, the novel, it will be seen how unsatisfactory they are. Nor can we attribute the decadence of letters to the artificial propaganda of the Republicans, who adopted as their criteria of good writing the qualities of high morality and democracy. For have we not observed in the works of novelists, from Marmontel till the Revolution, ample indication that the only thing that mattered to these writers was the morality of the novel, which degenerated as a genre just because of this subordination of probability to moral utility. Nor was evidence wanting to show that old prejudices were breaking down, and that a democratic spirit was already permeating this form of literature. M. Hazard quotes the Republican *Décade* of the year III as saying: "In general we had scarcely any good novels in French. . . . The authors worked only for the nobility. As a result they portrayed foibles rather than passions, miniatures rather than pictures. One found in them very little truth, and few of those truths which belong to all men and can be recognised and felt by all." It would be scarcely necessary to point out the fallacy of this, a fallacy which M. Hazard is of course too acute a critic to ignore, were it not that M. Hazard seems to sponsor the opinions expressed by the *Décade* when, in common with other critics, he alleges the emigration of the nobility and the breaking up of the *salons* as reasons for the decay of belles-lettres. But, as we are obliged to repeat, such arguments have no valid application to the novel, which degenerated for quite other reasons, one of which was the subordination of the probability of the novel to the intellectual propaganda of the habitués of those *salons* which, in M. Hazard's opinion, "pronounced decrees on good taste." Again, the novelist did not write exclusively for the nobility: on the contrary, the majority of his readers belonged to the middle classes, in particular to the provincials, a fact which several eighteenth-century critics refer to scornfully, in order to depreciate the novel as a genre. As for the effect of the emigration on the standard of the nation's literature, it is obvious that we are now dealing with pure conjecture. It is possible, of course, that the budding genius of an unknown Balzac was prevented from flowering by the chill unfriendliness of a foreign atmosphere, yet a Chateaubriand and a Mme de Staël throve well under this enforced transplanting.

The decay of the novel at the close of the century was not due to the political upheavals, though the causes which produced it are obscurely entangled in those which brought about the Revolution. The last decade of the eighteenth century marks the supersession of objectivism by subjectivism in the novel. The novelist, ever since Rousseau, had been turning his gaze from the external world to the world within himself. To the seventeenth-century novelist the "proper study of mankind" was man in general. The eighteenth-century writer, whilst still maintaining the same objective standpoint, interested himself, not in man, but in individuals, and thereby disclosed a fascinating array of new facts and ideas. With Rousseau and the pre-Romantics this objective individualism, if we may call it so, tended to become more and more subjective, and already in Rétif, a mediocre writer it is true, we have an example of the application of a new conception of the function of the novelist, who regards individuals only in relation to his ego. Henceforth, until the advent of the great realist and objective school of 1850, the novel was to be a "confession," but not, as in Rétif, a recital of sordid, physical adventures. In the fourth year of the new century Chateaubriand, heralding that glorious florescence which we call Romanticism, revealed in the splendid indiscretion of his *René*, the ineffable melancholy of a noble soul tortured by that *mal du siècle* for which there is no logical remedy save death.

INDEX

The principal references are indexed in black figures